ROADMAP™ A2

WORKBOOK

Damian Williams

CONTENTS

1A

Grammar

Verb be – positive and negative

1 Choose the correct alternatives.

1 This *is/are* Pippa.
2 I*'m/'re* from Scotland.
3 They *isn't/aren't* from the US.
4 You*'s/'re* in class 3C.
5 James *is/am* 27 years old.
6 My brother *isn't/aren't* a teacher.
7 John and Carrie *are/is* from the UK.
8 The pizza *not is/isn't* very good.

2 Correct the mistake in each sentence.

1 Gin and Ken ~~is~~ *are* from Scotland.

2 Pedro aren't from Argentina. He's from Brazil.

3 My name am Anna. I'm from the Frankfurt office.

4 Where is you from?

5 I think they Vietnamese.

6 We's Australian, not British.

7 My town are about 30 kilometres from Warsaw.

8 John and Trina is from the same town.

9 It are nice to meet you.

10 She am not a student.

3 Make the positive sentences negative and the negative sentences positive.

1 Karen isn't from Nigeria.
   Karen's from Nigeria.
2 They aren't in my class.

3 I'm not from London.

4 It's our first time here.

5 They're students.

6 It isn't cold in here.

7 I'm happy.

8 You are very tall.

Vocabulary

Countries and nationalities

4 Choose the correct alternatives.

1 He's from *the US/American*.
2 They're *China/Chinese*.
3 I'm *Türkiye/Turkish*.
4 We're from *Australia/Australian*.
5 She's from *Egypt/Egyptian*.
6 He isn't *Poland/Polish*.
7 Her father's *Greece/Greek*.
8 They aren't *Brazil/Brazilian*.
9 I'm from *Japan/Japanese*.
10 We aren't American. We're from *Russia/Russian*.

5 Write the nationalities for the countries 1–8.

1 Australia _____
2 Greece _____
3 Spain _____
4 Japan _____
5 Mexico _____
6 China _____
7 Russia _____
8 Egypt _____

6 Complete the conversations with a country or nationality in Exercises 4 or 5.

1 **A:** I think she's from Spain.
   B: No, she isn't. She's M_____ .
2 **A:** I'm from G_____ .
   B: Oh wow! I'm G_____ , too!
3 **A:** We're from P_____ .
   B: Nice to meet you. We're C_____ .
4 **A:** This is Kiko. She's from J_____ .
   B: Nice to meet you, Kiko. I'm Dalilah. I'm from
   E_____ .
5 **A:** Where are you from?
   B: I'm from R_____ .

Vocabulary
Question words

1 Choose the correct alternatives.

1 A: *Who's/ What's* your teacher's name?
   B: It's Brian, I think.

2 A: *Where/ When* is the party?
   B: At the school.

3 A: *When/ What* is Jo's birthday?
   B: Next week.

4 A: *Who/ How* is he?
   B: My sister's boyfriend.

5 A: *How/ Who* is he?
   B: He's OK, thanks.

6 A: *Are/ How* you OK?
   B: Yes, I'm OK.

7 A: *What's/ Where's* your favourite food?
   B: I love Japanese food!

6 A: *When/ Is* it time to go?
   B: Yes, it is.

2 Complete the questions with the correct word.

1 .... is Tom today? Is he OK?
2 .... is the lesson today? Room 5?
3 .... you a new student?
4 .... is the lesson? 2 p.m.?
5 .... is your new phone number?
6 .... is your favourite person?
7 .... time is it?
8 .... old are you?

Grammar
Questions with *be*

3 Match questions 1–8 with answers a–h.

1 Are you a student?   a Patricia.
2 What's your name?   b No, they aren't.
3 Is she from China?   c Yes, I am.
4 Where's our class?   d Yes, it is!
5 Are they shop assistants?   e We're on Goodge Street, I think.
6 Where are we?   f No, she isn't.
7 When's the class?   g It's in room 6B.
8 Is it cold?   h It's on Tuesday.

4 Put the words in the correct order to make questions.

1 you / on / Are / the / course / Chinese / ?
   Are you on the Chinese course?

2 email / your / What's / address / ?
   ....

3 the / When / classes / are / ?
   ....

4 manager / Is / the / she / ?
   ....

5 today / are / How / you / ?
   ....

6 you / in / photography / Are / interested / ?
   ....

7 birthday / is / When / your / ?
   ....

8 a / Are / assistant / you / shop / ?
   ....

9 Is / home / Harry / at / ?
   ....

10 from / Where / teacher / your / is / ?
   ....

5 Write questions with *be* for the answers.

1 My phone number is 07956 76430128.
   What's your phone number?

2 I'm a dentist.
   ....

3 Paulo's at home.
   ....

4 They're from Mexico.
   ....

5 My favourite food is sushi.
   ....

6 The classes are at 8 p.m.
   ....

7 I'm in class 4b.
   ....

8 Sheila isn't here.
   ....

Vocabulary

Everyday objects 1

1 **Complete the words for everyday objects.**

1 r_ng	6 l_pt_p
2 sk_t_b_ _rd	7 t_nn_s r_ck_t
3 s_ngl_ss_s	8 c_m_r_
4 b_ _rd g_m_s	9 _mbr_ll_
5 b_k_	10 p_ct_r_

2 **Which of the objects in Exercise 1 are for ...**

* studying?

  ....

* playing/sport?

  ....

  ....

* wearing?

  ....

3 **Choose the correct alternatives.**

1 A: Let's play a *board game*/*clock*.

   B: OK, which one?

2 A: Wow, that's a nice *umbrella*/*bike*!

   B: Yes, I ride it every day!

3 A: Is that *picture*/*laptop* fast?

   B: Yes, it is.

4 A: Is that a new *camera*/*laptop*?

   B: Yes, it takes great pictures!

Grammar

this, *that*, *these* and *those*

4 **Complete the table with *this*, *that*, *these* or *those*.**

	near	far
singular	1 .... *this*	2 ....
plural	3	4 ....

5 **Choose the correct alternatives.**

1 A: What's *this*/*that* over there?

   B: It's my bike.

2 A: Are *this*/*those* your sunglasses?

   B: No, *these*/*those* are my sunglasses here.

3 A: Hi, James. *This*/*These* is Suki.

   B: Hi, Suki. Nice to meet you.

4 A: I like *that*/*those* bag.

   B: Ooh, me too. It's nice.

5 A: How much is *that*/*those* clock?

   B: *This*/*That* one here?

   A: No, *this*/*that* one over there.

   B: It's £50.

6 A: Excuse me, are *these*/*those* your bags over there?

   B: No, our bags are here.

6 **Use the prompts and *this*, *that*, *these* or *those* to write sentences and questions.**

1 sunglasses / from Italy. (near)

   These sunglasses are from Italy. ....

2 your bike? (far)

   ....

3 picture / nice. (near)

   ....

4 Mike / over there? (far)

   ....

5 How much / book? (far)

   ....

6 Hi, Sundeep. / Ben. (near)

   ....

7 How much / board games? (near)

   ....

8 bag / £50. (near)

   ....

9 your pen? (near)

   ....

10 lamp / not Chinese. (far)

   ....

Functional language
Tell the time

1 **Match the sentence halves.**

1 What's the	a quarter to four.
2 It's a	b is it there?
3 It's nine	c time in New Zealand?
4 What time	d past two in the morning.
5 It's half	e o'clock.

2 **Choose the correct alternatives.**

1 **A:** What time *is it / it is* now?
   B: It's *a half / half* past three.
2 **A:** What's *a / the* time?
   B: It's two *o'clock / hour*.
3 **A:** What *'re / 's* the time in Glasgow?
   B: It's a *fifteen / quarter* past six.
4 **A:** *What / What's* time is it in Montreal?
   B: It's *four and twenty / four twenty* p.m.
5 **A:** What's the time *there / is it*?
   B: It's half *to / past* nine.
6 **A:** What time is it *in / at* New York?
   B: It's four *a.m. / in the a.m.*

3 **Write the time in two ways.**

1 4.20 *It's four twenty.* / *It's twenty past four.*
2 9.45 .... / ....
3 1.30 .... / ....
4 7.55 .... / ....
5 5.30 .... / ....
6 2.25 .... / ....
7 3.15 .... / ....
8 11.35 .... / ....

Listening

1 🔊 **1.01** **Listen to three conversations. Match conversations 1–3 with places a–c.**

a a dance class ....
b a conference ....
c at work ....

2 **Listen again and tick the countries and nationalities that you hear.**

Italy	Italian
Spain	Spanish
Russia	Russian
Australia	Australian
Greece	Greek
the US	American
China	Chinese
the UK	British
Mexico	Mexican

3a **Are the sentences true (T) or false (F)?**

1 Today is Carla's first day. ....
2 Rob is Spanish. ....
3 Skyler and Joanne are both Australian. ....
4 They work in the Sydney office. ....
5 This is Miguel's first salsa class. ....
6 Miguel and Claudia are from the same city in Mexico. ....

b **Listen again and check.**

4 **Match the words in bold in 1–4 with meanings a–d.**

1 This is Carla, our new **staff member**. ....
2 Can you **introduce** her ... .
3 ... to the **team**, please. ....
4 What **department** are you in? ....

a group of people who work together
b somebody who works in a place
c part of a company
d tell people another person's name

Reading

1 **Read the advertisements 1–4 and match them with titles a–d.**

a Study English in New York ....

b English in the beautiful countryside ....

c English Anywhere ....

d Learn English in only six months! ....

2 **Read the advertisements again and answer the questions.**

Which English course (1–4) ...

a includes other types of classes? ....

b is good for making friends? ....

c is quick? ....

d has games? ....

e has small classes? ....

f is in a quiet place? ....

g is completely online? ....

3 **Read the advertisements again. Are the sentences true (T) or false (F)?**

1 Course 1 is the same as other courses. ....

2 It's good for people with not much time. ....

3 Course 2 is in a city. ....

4 There are swimming classes in the morning. ....

5 Course 3 is in a big city. ....

6 There are classes all day. ....

7 Course 4 is in a big school. ....

8 Vira enjoys her course. ....

4 **Match the words in the box with meanings 1–5.**

boating   exciting   improve   lake   social programme

1 become better at something

....

2 a plan of free-time activities

....

3 makes you feel happy/ interested

....

4 a big area of water, not the sea

....

5 using a small boat for fun

....

1

Are you busy?

Do you need to learn English fast?

Well, don't worry, *English Maximum* is for you.

Our way of teaching is new, exciting and . . . fast.

You can speak English in six months.

Join us today!

2

Leave the work and noise of the city and join us in the quiet English countryside. Our school is in the Lake District, a beautiful area in the north of England.

In the morning, there are English classes with our excellent teachers.

In the afternoon, there are sports classes for everyone, in and around the lake. These include

- tennis   - yoga   - boating   - swimming
- and many, many more.

3

- Study with us in the city that never sleeps. We have many different types of English classes in the morning, afternoon and evening, with no more than six students in each class.

- Our social programme is excellent because there are so many things to do in this exciting city, like a trip to the Statue of Liberty or a picnic in Central Park.

- Our teachers are interesting and can help you succeed. This is the place for you!

4

With our website and mobile app, you can study English anywhere: at home, at work or on the bus! Our new 100% online system is fun, with games and exercises to help you improve all the time.

'I'm a manager in a large office, and I'm very busy. But with *English Anywhere* I study a little every day. It's great fun!'

Vira, manager

Writing

1 Read the online competition entry. What do they want you to write about? What else do they want?

ONLINE SHOW & TELL

What's your favourite object?
Tell us what it is and why it's special to you.
Send us a photo and your description and you can win £50!

2 Read Clara's description and answer the questions.
1 Where is her suitcase from?
2 How old is it?
3 Why does she like it?
4 What is the name of her suitcase?
5 Is it a large suitcase?

This is my favourite object. It's a Brazilian suitcase and it's from São Paulo, from a shop in Oscar Freire Street. This is a fashionable street in the city. It's ten years old and it's special because it goes everywhere with me. It's quite small, but that's OK. I like it so much it has a name – its name is Sandra!

3 Read the Focus box. Find examples in Clara's description of each use of capital letters.

Using capital letters and full stops

A sentence has a subject and a verb. We use capital letters (e.g. A, B, C) at the beginning of a sentence. We use a full stop (.) at the end of a sentence.
He's a big music fan.

Sometimes a phrase makes a sentence, but there's no subject or verb. These phrases start with a capital letter and end with a full stop.
Hi, everyone. Welcome to the group.

We also use capital letters for:
• the subject *I*
• people's names
• road or street names
• names of towns, cities, states and countries
• nationalities
• languages
• names of companies and universities
• days and months

4 Rewrite Abdul's description with 12 capital letters and 5 full stops.

these are my board games i love playing them with my friends every wednesday evening we play them together at a club in woodhall university on green street they are all english my friend raed is very good at them

....
....
....
....
....

Prepare

5 You're going to write a description of a special object for the competition. Choose an object and make notes on these things:
• What is it?
• What is its name (if any)?
• Where is it from?
• How old is it?
• Is it big or small?
• Is it cheap or expensive?

Write

6 Write your description. Use your notes in Exercise 5 and the Focus box to help you.

Vocabulary

Family members

1 Complete the words for family members.

1 f _ _ h e _
2 _ a _ e _ t _
3 _ a u _ h _ _ r
4 _ u _
5 c _ i _ _ r e _
6 g _ _ n _ _ a _ _ e _
7 _ r _ _ d m _
8 _ o _

2 Complete the table with the words in Exercise 1.

Male	Female	Both
father		

3 Complete the sentences.

1 My mother is my _____ *mum* _____ .
2 My grandson and my granddaughter are my
_____ .
3 My father's brother is my _____ .
4 My mum and my dad are my _____ .
5 My son and my daughter are my _____ .
6 My grandmother is married to my _____ .
7 My sister's son is my _____ .
8 My grandfather and my grandmother are my
_____ .

Grammar

Possessive adjectives and possessive 's

4 Put the possessive *'s* in the correct place in each sentence.

1 John is Alice∧grandad.   *'s*

2 Vera and Alfie are Mark grandparents.

3 My parents house is quite big.

4 My dad dad is called Harry.

5 What's your mother name?

6 Is Kira Jean-Luc sister?

7 Her son name is Chris.

8 Is that Briana bike?

9 My grandparents dog is called Poppy.

10 My brother name is Damiano.

5 Choose the correct alternatives.

1 **A:** Is this *your/you're* pen?
   B: No, it's *Rachel/Rachel's*.
2 **A:** What's your *brother is/brother's* name?
   B: *He's/His* name is Luke.
3 **A:** Is *Stan Michelle's/Stan's Michelle* grandad?
   B: No, he's *her/his* uncle.
4 **A:** Who's Margaret?
   B: Margaret is *Brian's/Brian* mum.
5 **A:** Are these *you're/your* keys?
   B: No, they're *Tanya's/Tanya* keys.
6 **A:** What's *your/you're* mum's name?
   B: *Its/It's* Beth.

6 Complete the text with the correct possessive adjectives.

> ¹ _____ family is quite small. I have one sister, and
> ² _____ name is Svetlana. We have a dog and
> ³ _____ name is Darya. My father has one brother,
> my uncle. ⁴ _____ name is Slava. ⁵ _____
> grandparents are very nice. ⁶ _____ daughters,
> (my aunts), live near us. What about ⁷ _____ family?
> Is it big or small?

Vocabulary
Everyday objects 2

1 **Put the letters in the correct order to make words for everyday objects.**
   1 supre   *purse*
   2 grinvid cleicen
   3 wearset
   4 neohp grachre
   5 shurbrahi
   6 cleankec
   7 keam-pu
   8 ringsear
   9 botonkeo
   10 banghad
   11 slogev
   12 fracs

2 **Find the words in Exercise 1 in the word search.**

P	S	W	E	R	T	A	E	A	R	R	I	N	G	S
C	R	E	W	Q	N	O	T	E	B	O	O	K	G	S
S	W	E	A	T	E	R	N	O	T	O	O	S	K	S
H	A	N	B	D	C	V	O	R	S	T	I	P	P	J
E	C	K	L	A	K	E	E	P	U	G	E	R	H	C
H	A	R	L	I	L	U	P	S	A	R	F	P	O	H
H	A	N	D	B	A	G	J	X	D	R	I	V	N	A
H	A	I	R	B	C	U	S	H	K	A	B	L	E	R
W	A	I	S	T	E	M	A	K	U	P	H	A	C	G
G	O	V	E	L	M	A	K	E	U	P	A	S	H	E
P	G	L	O	V	E	S	F	I	O	U	S	W	A	H
U	S	W	E	T	R	E	I	E	A	R	E	I	R	A
R	U	N	H	A	I	R	B	R	U	S	H	T	G	N
D	R	I	V	I	N	G	L	I	C	E	N	C	E	D
S	U	C	H	U	S	H	A	R	F	S	C	A	R	F

3 **Which seven objects in the word search can you wear?**

Grammar
whose and possessive pronouns

4 **Choose the correct alternatives.**
   1 A: Is this your notebook?
      B: Yes, it's *my / mine*.
   2 A: Are those your earrings?
      B: No, they're *your / yours*!
   3 A: *Who's / Whose* are those gloves?
      B: They're *Jack's / Jack*.
   4 A: Is that Lianne's make-up?
      B: I don't think it's *her's / hers*.
   5 A: *Whose / Who's* phone charger is this?
      B: It's *ours / us*.

5 **Correct the mistake in eight of the sentences. Two sentences are correct.**
   1 This make-up is ~~they're~~.   *theirs*
   2 Those earrings are Sallys.
   3 Who's wallet is this?
   4 Is this sweater yours?
   5 This cap is mine, but that one's your.
   6 These gloves are my.
   7 Is this our?
   8 Whose necklace is this?
   9 These notebooks are their.
   10 This laptop charger is our's.

6 **Rewrite the sentences using a possessive pronoun.**
   1 They're Janice's earrings.   *They're hers* .
   2 That's James's skateboard.

   3 Is this your cap?

   4 It's Kate and Nathan's phone number.

   5 Are these my books?

   6 Those are your sunglasses.

   7 It's Fiona's handbag.

   8 Are they our sandwiches?

Vocabulary
Adjectives describing objects

1 Choose the correct alternatives.
1 I like your teddy bear. He's really *soft/broken*!
2 This is *an old/a modern* photo of my mum when she was a girl.
3 My laptop is *broken/useful*. I can't use it.
4 These books are very *special/soft* to me.
5 I love your earrings. They're very *beautiful/broken*!
6 My gloves are so *comfortable/round*. They feel lovely.
7 My new mobile is small, *heavy/light* and easy to use.
8 Do you prefer the square table or the *round/soft* one?
9 A vocabulary notebook is very *modern/useful*.
10 That's a beautiful *brown/gold* ring.

2 Complete the descriptions with the words in the box.

> bike   board game   earrings   laptop   umbrella

I've got a new **1**_____. It's very small, light and modern. It's useful for my work, but also in my free time it's useful to talk to my friends online.

I love my gold **2**_____. They're big, round and beautiful. I wear them every time I go out.

It's an old **3**_____, but it's always fun to play. It's special because I always have a good time when I play it with my family.

My dad always takes his **4**_____ to work. He hates getting wet!

I love my **5**_____. It's quite old now, but it's light and fast. I think it's beautiful and it's easy to ride.

3 Write the opposite of each adjective.
1 old   m_____
2 heavy   l_____
3 small   l_____

Grammar
have got

4 Choose the correct alternatives.
1 Dora *'s/'ve* got a new bike.
2 We *haven't/hasn't* got any gloves and it's cold!
3 *Have you/Do you have* got the wifi password?
4 No, they *hasn't/haven't* got a garden.
5 Er, no. I *not have got/haven't got* a pet.
6 She *'s/'ve* got a really comfortable new sofa.
7 *Has/Have* Kate and Andrew got a car?
8 Mark *have/has* got a job.
9 *Do we have/Have we* got any eggs?
10 They *not have/haven't* got any children.

5 Make the positive sentences negative and the negative sentences positive.
1 We've got a large car.
   We haven't got a large car.
2 Sara hasn't got a bag with her.
3 He hasn't got a car, but he's got a bike.
4 I've got a camera with me.
5 My flat hasn't got a garden.
6 I've got time now.

6 Use the prompts to write conversations.
1 A: you / a car?
   Have you got a car?
   B: No, / . But I / a bike.
   No, I haven't. But I've got a bike.
2 A: they / a garden?
   B: Yes, / .
3 A: she / any brothers or sisters?
   B: Yes, / . She / two brothers and one sister.
4 A: you / the password?
   B: No, / . Sorry.
5 A: Scott / any pets?
   B: Yes, / . He / a dog.

Functional language
Buy things in a shop

1 **Complete the conversations with the words in the box.**

> are   change   got   like   much

Customer: Have you ¹_____ any medicine for a cold?
Assistant: Yes, we have. How many packets would you ²_____?
Customer: Two, please. How ³_____ is that?
Assistant: That's £4.20, please.
Customer: Here you ⁴_____.
Assistant: That's 80 pence ⁵_____.
Customer: Thank you.

> else   Have   where

Customer: ⁶_____ you got any books about French cooking?
Assistant: Yes, of course. They're on the second floor.
Customer: Great, thanks. And ⁷_____ do I pay?
Assistant: Just over there, by the door. Anything ⁸_____?
Customer: No thanks.

> Can   Cash   Would

Assistant: Hi, can I help you?
Customer: ⁹_____ I have a small cappuccino and a cheese sandwich, please?
Assistant: Sure. Anything else?
Customer: No thanks.
Assistant: ¹⁰_____ or card?
Customer: Card.
Assistant: OK, that's £4.75, please. ¹¹_____ you like a bag?
Customer: No thanks, I've got my own.

2 **Match the sentence halves.**

1	Can I pay	a	else?
2	Anything	b	are these shoes?
3	Here	c	a bag?
4	Can I have	d	pay?
5	Would you like	e	£8.25, please.
6	Cash	f	by card?
7	How much	g	you are.
8	That's	h	a small cola, please?
9	How many	i	bottles would you like?
10	Where do I	j	or card?

3 **Who says each phrase in Exercise 2: the customer (C) or the assistant (A)?**

1 ___   2 ___   3 ___   4 ___   5 ___   6 ___
7 ___   8 ___   9 ___   10 ___

Listening

1 🔊 **2.01 Listen to a podcast about families and answer the questions.**
   1 Who is Russell's favourite family member?
   2 Who is Jeanette's favourite?

2 **Listen again. Are the statements true for Russell (R), Jeanette (J) or both (B)?**
   1 He/She has got a big family. ___
   2 He/She has got lots of brothers and sisters. ___
   3 He/She hasn't got any brothers or sisters. ___
   4 He/She talks about his/her parents' jobs. ___
   5 He/She has got lots of uncles and aunts. ___
   6 He/She lives in the same area as his/her family. ___

3a **Choose the correct alternatives.**
   1 There are *ten/eleven* people and one pet in Russell's family.
   2 Russell's *mum/dad* works in an office.
   3 He's got *three/four* sisters.
   4 Jeanette's dad has got *two/four* brothers and sisters.
   5 She's got ten *children/cousins*.
   6 She *likes/doesn't like* her family.

 b **Listen again and check.**

4 **Match the words in bold 1–3 with meanings a–c.**
   1 ... something both of my **guests** know all about. ___
   2 And then I've got seven **siblings** ... ___
   3 And they've all got **kids**, you see. ___

   a brothers and sisters
   b children
   c people you invite

Reading

1 Read the advertisement for a website. Who is it for?

a people who have got old things they don't want any more

b people who need things they haven't got

c both

2 Read the advertisement again. Answer the questions.

1 What objects are in the first paragraph?

....

....

2 What three types of people might need these objects?

....

....

3 What's the name of the website?

....

4 How much is it to use the website?

....

5 What four adjectives does the advert use to describe the website?

....

....

6 How many people use the website?

....

3 Read the advertisement again. Are the sentences true (T) or false (F)?

1 An engineer might need a printer. ....

2 The website is new. ....

3 You only need to post a photo of something you offer. ....

4 You need to email members that have something you want. ....

5 Using the website is difficult. ....

4 Match the words/phrases in bold in the advertisement with meanings 1–7.

1 to phone, email or write to spmeone

....

2 things which connect electronic devices

....

3 a large seat for more than one person

....

4 put something on a website

....

5 not working ....

6 instructions ....

7 people in a group ....

Have you got what I need?

You've got lots of things you don't want at home: some old **cables**, a **broken** printer, maybe even something big like a **sofa** and chairs? You want them out of your house.

Wait! Maybe someone else needs them. Maybe an engineer lost the cables for their laptop. Maybe there's a student who needs a printer.

Maybe there's a young person in a new home who needs furniture?

Introducing *clearitfindit.com*. Whether you've got something you don't need or you need something you haven't got, *clearitfindit.com* is the site for you. Just follow these easy **steps**.

Offers:

1 Take a photo of your object.

2 Write a description.

3 **Post** it on the website.

Needed:

1 Read the posts on the website.

2 See something you need.

3 **Contact** the person by email.

This new website is free, easy to use and useful. Thousands of people are **members** already. Join us today and make your life clean and tidy again!

Writing

1 Complete the descriptions with the objects in the box.

bike   laptop   notebook   scarf

lost property form

A Description of object:

This is a _____ . It's small and square. It's brown and it's got the letters DW on the front. It's not expensive, but it's very important to me. I'm a writer and I write all my notes and ideas in it, so it's important for my work.

B Description of object:

Lost _____ ! I have lots of exams to study for, so I need to find it. It's a 'Factbook' and it's silver and blue.

C Description of object:

It's a beautiful _____ . It's green and it's very soft and comfortable. It's cold now, so I need it to keep warm!

D Description of object:

It's a large men's _____ . It's green and black and very fast. It's not new, but it's expensive. I use it to go to work every day and I don't have a car, so I need to find it.

2 Read the Focus box. Underline examples of the linkers in descriptions B, C and D in Exercise 1.

Using *and, but* and *so*

Use *and, but* and *so* to join two ideas or sentences.

and = add information

    +   +
It's <u>small</u> and <u>square</u>.

but = give opposite or different information

        –   +
It's <u>not expensive</u>, but it's <u>very important to me</u>.

so = give a result

I'm a writer and <u>I write all my notes and ideas in it</u>, so <u>it's important for my work</u>.

3 Join sentences 1–6 with sentences a–f using a linker.

1 It's not expensive.
  It's not expensive, but it's important to me.
2 It's cold now.
  _____
3 They're gold.
  _____
4 My bike is large.
  _____
5 My laptop is broken.
  _____
6 They're not beautiful.
  _____

a They're beautiful.
b It's not useful.
c It's important to me.
d They're comfortable.
e My bike is heavy.
f I need my sweater.

Prepare

4a You're going to write three descriptions of objects for a lost property office. First choose three objects, then make notes on these things for each object:
• adjectives to describe it
• why it's important to you/what you need it for
• any other useful information

b Think about how you can use linkers in your description.

Write

5 Write your descriptions. Use your notes in Exercise 4a and the Focus box to help you.

Vocabulary

Free-time activities 1

1 Complete the phrases with the verbs in the box.

| cook do go (x2) meet paint/draw play read |
| visit watch |

1 .... books/a newspaper
2 .... friends
3 .... with our children
4 .... sport
5 .... food/dinner
6 .... online
7 .... for a bike ride/for coffee/for a walk
8 .... TV/sport on TV
9 .... pictures
10 .... a museum

2 Choose the correct alternatives.

1 My favourite free-time activity is when I *play/meet* with my children at the weekend.
2 When my friends come round to my house we *see/watch* sport on TV.
3 It's a lovely day outside. Let's *do/go* for a walk.
4 Alexandru likes to *read/watch* a newspaper while he has breakfast.
5 In the evenings, I usually *play/meet* friends or go to the gym.
6 Why don't we go to London and *watch/visit* a museum?
7 It's not fair! I always *go/cook* dinner in our house.
8 *Go/Do* online and find something to do for free near here.

3 Complete the text with phrases in Exercise 1.

Every weekend, I **1**............... friends and we do
something together. We might **2**............... a museum,
3............... for a coffee or just **4**............... TV
together. My favourite friend is Frances. We're the same
age and she's an artist. She likes to **5**...............
pictures of animals and she's very good. We both
6............... a lot of books and we like the same kinds,
so we always talk about them together. Sometimes
I **7**............... dinner for friends at home. I really like
cooking. Whatever we do, we always have a good
time together.

Grammar

Present simple with *I, you, we* and *they*; adverbs of frequency and time expressions

4 Correct the mistake in each sentence.

 often go
1 I g̶o̶ ̶o̶f̶t̶e̶n̶ out with friends.

2 We not watch TV in the morning.

3 You don't never cook on Fridays.

4 The children are go online in the evening.

5 We visit a museum once on a month.

6 You have always pizza!

7 I cook dinner for my family night every.

8 They not have a lot of free time.

9 We often are do a lot of sport.

10 I read rarely newspapers – I don't have time!

5 Put the words in the correct order to make sentences.

1 at / I / go / weekend / the / out / often / .
  I often go out at the weekend.
2 watch / We / TV / on / rarely / sport / .
  ....
3 cook / sometimes / dinner / You / .
  ....
4 every / They / walk / a / day / for / go / .
  ....
5 lot / I / a / of / books / read / .
  ....
6 TV / afternoon / the / rarely / I / in / watch / .
  ....
7 make / dinner / They / for / pasta / often / .
  ....
8 Saturday / grandma / meet / I / every / my / .
  ....
9 a lot of / at the / weekend / We / have / don't / free time / .
  ....
10 go / the evenings / I / ever / online / hardly / in / .
  ....

3B

Vocabulary
Everyday activities

1 **Choose the correct alternatives.**

1 *do/go* to bed
2 *get/go* ready
3 *have/do* my hair
4 *get/do* dressed
5 *get/have* a shower
6 *go/do* to work
7 *leave/go* to the gym
8 *go/get* up
9 *leave/start* home
10 *go/do* exercise
11 *start/play* work
12 *go/have* breakfast

2 **Match the sentence halves.**

1 I always do ....
2 We go to ....
3 I have ....
4 I don't always ....
5 Hayley finishes ....
6 I need some time to get ....
7 John has ....
8 I often get ....

a have breakfast.
b exercise at the weekend.
c dinner with his family at 9 p.m.
d home late in the week.
e bed early in the week.
f work early on Fridays.
g ready.
h a shower every morning.

3 **Complete the sentences with a verb in the correct form.**

1 We usually .... lunch around 1 p.m.
2 Marsha .... to the gym every day.
3 Greg .... his hair after breakfast in the morning.
4 We usually .... up late at the weekend.
5 They .... a shower every morning.
6 Hurry up and .... ready – we need to leave!
7 Phoebe .... dressed before she has breakfast.
8 I want to .... to bed early tonight. I'm tired.
9 We .... home at 7 a.m. and get the bus.

Grammar
Present simple with *he, she* and *it*

4 **Correct the mistake in each sentence.**

     watches
1 Sara ~~watchs~~ TV every evening.

2 She get ups early in the morning.

3 Paulo don't have breakfast in the morning.

4 He carrys a big bag with him at work.

5 We plays video games together.

6 Sheena love her job.

7 I starts work at 9 a.m.

8 Chiara don't goes to the gym.

9 I like action films, but she don't like them.

10 We doesn't have dinner together.

5 **Complete the text with the present simple form of the verbs in brackets.**

Moyra **1**................ (get up) at 10 p.m. She **2**................ (not have) breakfast, but she **3**................ (have) a quick shower. She **4**................ (leave) home at 10.45 p.m. and **5**................ (get) to the police station at 11 p.m. where she **6**................ (start) work with her partner. She **7**................ (love) her job because every night is different. She **8**................ (have) lunch with her partner at the police station at 2 a.m. When she **9**................ (finish) work in the morning, she **10**................ (go) home to see her children before they **11**................ (start) school. She **12**................ (say) 'good morning' to them and they **13**................ (say) 'good night' to her!

3c

Grammar
Present simple questions

1 Complete the questions with *do* or *does*.
1 _____ you ever play video games?
2 _____ she go out at the weekend?
3 What time _____ Chris start work?
4 How often _____ they go to the gym?
5 Where _____ you work?
6 What time _____ she get up in the morning?
7 Where _____ he live?
8 Who _____ you play games online with?
9 How many times a year _____ you go to the theatre?
10 _____ he do any sport?

2 Complete the conversations with the missing words.
1 A: _____ you go to the gym?
   B: No, I _____. I prefer to run outside.
2 A: _____ she go to the cinema much?
   B: Yes, she _____. Every week!
3 A: _____ Phil and Karen ever go to concerts?
   B: Yes, they _____. Quite often, actually.
4 A: _____ your sister play the guitar?
   B: Yes, she _____. She's very good.
5 A: _____ Michael go out during the week?
   B: No, he _____. He prefers to stay in.

3 Write questions for the answers.
1 *How often do you go to the gym?*
   I go to the gym <u>every day</u>.
2 _____
   Alessandra lives in <u>Rio de Janeiro</u>.
3 _____
   She's <u>36 years old</u>.
4 _____
   We <u>go out or cook food</u> at the weekend.
5 _____
   She meets friends <u>at a local café</u>.
6 _____
   John works <u>in a bank</u>.
7 _____
   My favourite food is <u>pasta</u>.
8 _____
   He's <u>a mechanic</u>.
9 _____
   No, I'm not <u>interested in football</u>.
10 _____
   My favourite actor is <u>Joaquin Phoenix</u>.

Vocabulary
Free-time activities 2

4 Cross out the activity that does not go with the verb.
1 **play** *video games/the radio/the guitar/games online*
2 **listen to** *the radio/a song/music/the theatre*
3 **watch** *the piano/a football match/TV/a film*
4 **go** *to the theatre/to the cinema/games online/to a concert*

5 Choose the correct alternatives.
1 How often do you *play/watch* football on TV?
2 I always *listen/listen to* music in the car.
3 I try to *go/visit* a museum once a month.
4 She *listens to/plays* games online.
5 Let's *go to/go* the theatre tonight.
6 Do you *watch/see* videos online?
7 John and Gina *watch/go to* the cinema every weekend.
8 Do you ever *listen to/watch* TV in the evening?

6 Complete the sentences with a verb in the correct form.
1 For my birthday I want to _____ to the theatre.
2 When do you usually _____ video games?
3 How often do they _____ games online?
4 She _____ her friends for coffee every Saturday.
5 Let's _____ to a concert this weekend.
6 She _____ TV every evening.
7 They _____ books every night before bed.
8 How often do you _____ to the cinema?

18

Functional language

Buy tickets

1 **Choose the correct alternatives.**

A: How **1**_can / do_ I help you?

B: I'd **2**_want / like_ two tickets for _Romeo and Juliet_, please.

A: **3**_Which / Whe_n time would you like?

B: 2 p.m., please.

A: I'm sorry, the 2 p.m. is sold **4**_full / out_.

B: Oh, OK. What about the 7.30 p.m.?

A: Let me see … yes, there are still some **5**_available / sold_.

B: Great!

A: Where do you want to **6**_play / sit_?

B: Near **7**_the / a_ front, please.

A: OK, no problem. That's sixty pounds, please.

B: OK.

A: Here you **8**_are / is_ – two tickets for _Romeo and Juliet_ at 7.30 p.m. Enjoy the show.

B: Thank you!

2 **Complete the conversation with the words in the box.**

> aren't   Here   much   that's   tickets
> together

A: Hi, how **1**................................ is a ticket for the Manchester United game on Saturday?

B: They're fifty pounds each.

A: OK, I'd like two **2**................................ then, please.

B: Do you want to sit **3**................................ ?

A: Yes, please.

B: Oh, I'm sorry, there **4**................................ any seats together. I can put you near each other though.

A: Um … OK then.

B: OK, **5**................................ a hundred pounds, please.

A: OK.

B: **6**................................ you are.

A: Thank you.

Listening

1 🔊 3.01 **Listen to an interview with a skiing champion. What does he do on Sunday?**

2 **Listen again. Put the things he does in the order that he usually does them in the week.**

a   He replies to emails.   ....

b   He skis.   ....

c   He gets up.   ....

d   He goes to bed.   ....

e   He has breakfast.   ....

f   He watches TV.   ....

g   He goes to the gym.   ....

h   He has lunch.   ....

3a **Choose the correct option, a or b.**

1   He's got .... medals.
    a   two   b   five

2   He does a few things at home .... he goes to the gym.
    a   before   b   after

3   He has chicken .... fish for lunch.
    a   and   b   or

4   He skis ....
    a   in the week.   b   at the weekend.

5   He watches TV ....
    a   before he goes to bed.   b   in bed.

b **Listen again and check.**

4 **Match the words in bold 1–4 with meanings a–d.**

1   … the American skier who's got three silver **medals** and two gold **medals**.   ....

2   I usually have an **omelette** and some coffee.   ....

3   … then I do a few **chores** at home.   ....

4   I think it's important for your body to **recover**.   ....

a   small jobs in the house

b   things you win in a sports competition

c   become well again

d   a dish made of eggs

Reading

1 **Read the article quickly. What's it about?**
a working from home
b different sleep patterns
c going to bed early

2 **Read the article again. Are the sentences true (T) or false (F)?**
1 Sarah and Jess think they have a problem. ....
2 Jess often sleeps late at the weekend. ....
3 Sarah gets up before Jess at the weekend. ....
4 Sarah works in an office. ....
5 Sarah prefers to work in the afternoon. ....
6 Sarah can think of new things in the morning. ....
7 Jess wakes up late because she goes to bed late. ....
8 Sarah reads in bed at night. ....

3 **Read the article again and complete the sentences with *Sarah* or *Jess*.**
1 .... gets up early.
2 .... often works at the weekend.
3 .... really likes sleeping.
4 .... goes to sleep quickly.
5 .... goes to sleep after doing something else.

4 **Look at the underlined words. Choose the option which has a similar meaning.**
1 She often has a lie-in until twelve! (paragraph 1)
   a She wakes up late.
   b She goes to bed late.
2 Our sleep patterns are very different. (paragraph 1)
   a the times we wake up and go to sleep
   b the hours we sleep
3 Jess falls asleep (paragraph 2)
   a starts sleeping
   b goes to bed
4 But Sarah and Jess are siblings (paragraph 3)
   a parents
   b brothers/sisters

Sleeping differently

Do you like an early night? Do you like to sleep late? What is it like in your home?

'Jess is definitely a good sleeper,' says Sarah. 'At the weekend, she often has a lie-in until twelve!' Sarah prefers to go to bed early and get up early in the morning, usually around 5 a.m. She works from home, often at the weekend. That's why she does a lot of work in the morning so she can enjoy the afternoon. 'I like it when Jess is asleep, because I know she loves it so much,' says Sarah. 'Our sleep patterns are very different, but it works for us. I like to work early in the morning. That's when I get my best ideas.'

So why does Jess wake up late? 'Well, it's not because I go to bed late,' explains Jess. 'Basically, I just really like my sleep!' Jess falls asleep as soon as she goes to bed, but Sarah doesn't. She usually reads for about an hour then she falls asleep.

Some people just need a lot of sleep and some people don't need much sleep at all. But Sarah and Jess are siblings who seem very happy living together.

Writing

1 Read Sasha's description of a typical weekend. What night does she go out with friends?

Nuckford University

University life isn't just about studying, of course. Here, some of our students describe their typical weekend.

Sasha A typical weekend for most students here at Nuckford University starts on a Friday night. Most students go out with friends and have a good time after studying all week, but I don't. On Friday evenings, I don't go out. I stay in and go to bed early. I play football for the university team and on Saturday mornings, we practise for about three hours. In the afternoon, I watch TV or a film then phone my mum for a chat.

On Saturday evening, I go out with my friends. We usually go to the university café to have dinner. It's not very exciting, but we like it because it's cheap! After that, we sometimes go to a club or sometimes we go to my friends' house and talk. They all live together in the same house, but I live in the university accommodation.

Sundays are quiet. I study, watch TV and cook a meal. My favourite is my mum's pasta recipe. In the summer, I play football outside with friends. In the winter, I go to the gym. I usually go to bed early on Sunday so I'm ready for classes on Monday.

2 Read the description again and answer the questions.

1 What do most students do on Friday night?

2 Why does Sasha stay in on Friday night?

3 How long does she play football for on Saturday?

4 Who does she call on Saturday?

5 Why do Sasha and her friends go to the university café?

6 What does she do in the winter on Sundays?

3 Read the Focus box. Find more examples of these uses of commas and apostrophes in Sasha's description.

Using commas and apostrophes

Use commas and apostrophes to help the reader understand your ideas.

Use a comma (,)
- after a time expression at the beginning of a sentence
  On Saturday evening, I go out with my friends.
- in a list
  I study, watch TV and cook a meal.

Use an apostrophe (')
- in contractions to show that a letter is not there
  I don't go out. (do not)
  ... it's cheap! (It is)
- in possessives
  ... my mum's pasta recipe. (the pasta recipe of my mum)

A possessive plural noun is followed by ' without *s*.
My friends' house.

Note that the possessive adjective of *it* is *its* without an apostrophe.

4 Add a comma or an apostrophe to each sentence.

1 That's a nice cap.

2 I get up have a shower and make breakfast.

3 Those are Alices sunglasses.

4 My friends names are Claire and Vicki.

5 On Saturday mornings I sleep late.

6 I dont like fish.

Prepare

5 You're going to write a description of your typical week or weekend. First make notes to answer the questions.
- Do you go out? Where? Who with?
- What do you do when you stay in?
- Do you do any exercise or go to the gym?
- Do you work or study? When?
- Do you cook?

Write

6 Write your description. Use your notes in Exercise 5 and the Focus box to help you.

Vocabulary

Places in a city

1 Put the letters in the clues in the correct order to complete the crossword.

² s h o ³p s

Across
2 ~~sposh~~
4 steacl
5 fifosec
7 ploice notiast
8 raggae
9 maduits
11 sub natiots
12 nitar stontia

Down
1 treathe
3 stop cioffe
6 strops trence
10 rac prak

2 Match ten of the words in Exercise 1 with the descriptions.

1 You send letters there. ....
2 You buy things there. ....
3 You watch musicals there. ....
4 You travel by train there. ....
5 You travel by bus there. ....
6 It's a very, very old building. ....
7 You take your car there for repairs. ....
8 Famous football teams play there. ....
9 You can swim or exercise there. ....
10 People work at desks there. ....

Grammar

there is/are

3 Choose the correct alternatives.

I hate my town, it's really boring. There aren't ¹*a/any* cinemas or theatres and it's very small. There ²*'re/'s* a shop, but it's very small and there ³*isn't/aren't* any nice things in it. There are ⁴*a/any* lot of cars in the town, so there ⁵*'re/'s* a lot of air pollution. However, there are ⁶*some/any* nice parks near my house. I often play football there with my friends and there's ⁷*a/some* nice football pitch. I'd like to move to a big city though.

4 Put the words in the correct order to make sentences or questions.

1 any / town / There / aren't / my / in / offices / .
   There aren't any offices in my town.
2 some / house / There / my / near / are / shops / .
   ....
3 shops / village / Are / your / any / there / in / ?
   ....
4 a post office / There / isn't / near / me / .
   ....
5 town / There / a police station / isn't / my / in / .
   ....
6 your / Is / there / a train station / in / town / ?
   ....
7 There / shops / are / of / lot / a / .
   ....
8 over / There's / there / a garage / .
   ....
9 your / any / shops / good / Are / there / town / in / ?
   ....
10 Is / a car park / there / near / the bank / ?
   ....

5 Use the prompts to write sentences with *there is/are*.

1 lot / museums / London.
   There are a lot of museums in London.
2 not / places for young people.
   ....
3 cinema / my town.
   ....
4 not / police station / near here.
   ....
5 train station / next to my office.
   ....
6 not / theatre / my city.
   ....
7 not / garages / this area.
   ....

Vocabulary

Things in a home

1 **Correct the spelling mistake in each sentence.**

curtains
1 Open the ~~certains~~, it's dark in here.

2 There's a big spider in the bathe!

3 We need to buy new furnitur for our house.

4 The glasses are in that cubboard.

5 There's a bath, but there's isn't a shauwer.

6 I'm in the gaden.

7 Put your clothes in the wardrove.

8 The car is in the garadge.

2 **Complete the sentences with the words in the box.**

| cupboard | curtains | garage | shower | upstairs | wardrobe |

1 There are some glasses in the .... up there.
2 Why don't you open the ....? It's really dark in here.
3 There's a .... in the bathroom upstairs.
4 Come on! Let's go and look ....
5 We keep our bikes in the ....
6 My husband has his own .... for his clothes.

3 **Complete the sentences with the correct word.**

1 That shop sells really nice furniture for the g............... .
2 It's dark outside; close the c............... .
3 Put the coffee away in the c..............., please.
4 Dad's in the g............... with his car. He loves that car.
5 This f............... is old. We need to buy a new sofa and chairs.
6 The bathroom is d..............., near the kitchen.
7 I have lots of clothes in my w............... .
8 There's some cola in the f............... .

Grammar

Articles

4 **Choose the correct alternatives.**

1 I put the dishes in *the* / – cupboard.
2 There's *a* / *the* TV in the kitchen.
3 I've got *a* / *the* cat and a dog. *A* / *The* dog's name is Leo.
4 This is *a* / *an* useful book.
5 We often play tennis at *the* / – weekend.
6 This is – / *a* lovely car.
7 There's *a* / *the* really comfortable bed in *a* / *the* bedroom.
8 Can you open *a* / *the* curtains, please?
9 Jia works at – / *the* night.
10 It's *a* / – nice room, but I don't like *a* / *the* carpet.

5 **Complete the conversations with *a, the* or – (no article).**

1 **A:** Where are .... keys?
   B: They're in .... cupboard.
2 **A:** Is Poppy in .... garden?
   B: I don't know. Open .... curtains and look.
3 **A:** I've got two children – .... boy and .... girl.
   B: What's .... girl's name?
4 **A:** What time do you usually have .... dinner?
   B: Around seven o'clock in .... evening.
5 **A:** I really liked that house.
   B: Which one?
   A: .... one with .... big bedroom.

6 **Insert five definite articles and six indefinite articles into the text.**

a
We don't have big house, but it's really nice inside. There are two bedrooms: big one and small one. Big one is where I sleep and small one is spare room. Downstairs, there's living room and kitchen. Living room is really bright. But my favourite thing about my house is garden. It's really big and in summer I like to sit outside and listen to music.

4c

Vocabulary

Equipment

1 **Match words 1–6 with meanings a–f.**

1 backpack
2 batteries
3 mirror
4 can
5 blanket
6 map

a This has food inside.
b Carry things in this.
c These give you electricity.
d This helps you find places.
e You can see yourself in this.
f You sleep under this.

2 **Complete the table with the words in the box.**

boots ~~bowl~~ gloves hat knife sunglasses
warm clothes water bottle

Things you use to eat/drink	Things you wear
bowl	

3 **Complete the sentences with words in Exercises 1 and 2.**

1 Always wear a _____ in the desert to keep cool.
2 I need my _____ – it's really bright out here.
3 Can I see the _____ ? I think we're lost.
4 We need to wear _____ today – it's cold.
5 Put the keys in your _____ so they're safe.
6 Is there any water left in the _____ ? I'm thirsty.
7 The radio's dead. Have we got any more _____ ?
8 Can I have the _____ to sleep under?
9 Cook the _____ of beans on the fire.
10 Wear _____ to keep your hands warm.

Grammar

need + noun, *need* + infinitive with *to*

4 **Put the words in the correct order to make sentences.**

1 a / need / You / map / take / to / .
_____

2 some / eggs / We / need / .
_____

3 warm / I / clothes / some / need / .
_____

4 new / a / needs / She / laptop / .
_____

5 sleep / to / some / I / get / need / .
_____

6 to / a / We / fire / start / need / .
_____

7 batteries / I / some / need / .
_____

8 blanket / a / need / You / .
_____

9 to / soon / We / leave / need / .
_____

10 get / water / I / some / to / need / .
_____

5 **Choose the correct alternatives.**

1 I need *a/ to buy* new bag.
2 We need *some/ to* money.
3 James *need/ needs* some water.
4 I don't need *to/ a* leave yet.
5 I need *a/ some* AAA batteries.
6 You need *to tell/ tell* her you're sorry.
7 We need *a/ to check* map.
8 We need *a/ to* ask someone for help.

6 **Use the prompts to write sentences for each situation.**

1 I'm late today.
I / need / call my mother.
I need to call my mother.

2 Let's have a picnic.
We / need / buy / food.
_____

3 They have a new baby.
They / need / find / a new house.
_____

4 I start work at 6 a.m.
I / need / get up / early.
_____

5 He has exams tomorrow.
He / need / study.
_____

6 I'm rich.
I / not need / money.
_____

24

Functional language

Ask for information

1 Put the words in the correct order to make questions.

1 changing / the / are / Where / rooms / ?
  Where are the changing rooms?

2 the / What / close / museum / does / time / ?
  ....

3 the / free / museum / Is / ?
  ....

4 take / museum / Can / in / I / the / photos / ?
  ....

5 pay / Where / I / do / ?
  ....

6 does / end / What / the / time / film / ?
  ....

7 a / near / Is / here / there / bank / ?
  ....

8 any / here / near / Are / toilets / there / ?
  ....

9 is / How / ticket / a / much / ?
  ....

2 Match questions 1–7 with answers a–g.

1 Where's the gift shop? ....
2 What time does the next train to London leave? ....
3 Where do I pay? ....
4 Is there a café here? ....
5 Is the museum free? ....
6 How much is a ticket? ....
7 Can I take photos in the theatre? ....

a At half past ten.
b It's £5.
c Yes, there is. It's on the fourth floor.
d No, sorry, you can't.
e No, it isn't, sorry. It's £10 per person.
f It's near the museum exit.
g At the front of the shop.

3 Complete the conversations with the words in the box.

Can   How   Is   there   time

1 **A:** Are .... any towels in the changing rooms?
  B: Yes, there are. Help yourself.
2 **A:** What .... does the film finish?
  B: At six fifty-five.
3 **A:** .... much is a ticket?
  B: It's £20.
4 **A:** .... I take photos?
  B: Yes, you can.
5 **A:** .... there a toilet near here?
  B: Yes, it's downstairs.

Listening

1  **4.01 Listen to five people describing the place where they all live. Is it a small town or a big city?**

2 Listen again. Are the sentences true (T) or false (F)?
Speaker 1
1 He doesn't like the town. ....
2 He thinks it's a good place for families. ....
Speaker 2
3 She thinks it's an interesting town. ....
4 She doesn't want to live there. ....
Speaker 3
5 He doesn't think the public transport is good. ....
6 He's got a car. ....
Speaker 4
7 He thinks it's an interesting place. ....
8 He doesn't like his neighbours. ....
Speaker 5
9 She works in the town. ....
10 The big city is a long way away. ....

3a Choose the correct alternatives.
1 Speaker 1 says there *are/aren't* a lot of cars.
2 Speaker 2 says there *are some/aren't any* clubs.
3 Speaker 3 says there's one bus every *30 minutes/hour*.
4 Speaker 3 says you *don't need/need* to have a car there.
5 Speaker 4 thinks the people in the town are *quiet/friendly*.
6 Speaker 5 says there's a big city *30 minutes/an hour* away.

b Listen again and check.

4 Match the words in bold 1–3 with meanings a–c.
1 … and it's **safe** to walk around. ....
2 I can't wait to **move away**. ....
3 I've got great **neighbours** and we often meet and do things together. ....

a start living in a different place
b the opposite of *dangerous*
c people who live near you

Reading

1 **Read the article about an unusual town. Why is it unusual?**

a There aren't any cars.

b There isn't a school.

c Most people live in the same building.

d People don't live in buildings.

2 **Read the article again. Are the sentences true (T) or false (F)?**

1 Whittier is in Canada. ....

2 Around 200 people visit the town in the summer. ....

3 The weather is bad in the winter. ....

4 Almost everyone in the town lives together. ....

5 There's a school in the building. ....

6 You can drive to the town. ....

3 **Read the article again and choose the correct option, a or b.**

1 People visit Whittier in the summer ....
  a for work.   b on holiday.

2 In the winter, people live in the same building because it's .... inside.
  a warm   b cold

3 There .... a place to send letters in the building.
  a is   b isn't

4 Children .... go outside in the winter.
  a need to   b don't need to

5 Cars drive .... through the tunnel to the town.
  a one way   b both ways

4 **Match the words in bold in the article with meanings 1–4.**

1 This makes you warm inside in winter.

  ....

2 You can drive your car or walk under the ground through this.

  ....

3 big ships which take people on holiday, going to different places

  ....

4 people who live in a building, town, city, etc.

  ....

The city inside

Do you ever look outside your window in the morning, see that the weather's bad and decide to just stay in? There's a town called Whittier in Alaska, in the US, where people do exactly that every winter.

Whittier is a very small town with only around 200 **residents**. In the summer, there are a lot of tourists – around 700,000. During the summer, it is a busy tourist town: **cruise ships** stop there, people visit the countryside and it's all quite beautiful.

However, in the winter, it gets very cold and dark, so nearly all the residents live together in the same building. Because it's just one building, the **heating** is cheap. It's very big and there are lots of floors and apartments for people to stay warm in. But they don't just sleep there. There's also a post office, a doctor's, a police station, and even an inside park for children to play in. There isn't a school inside the building though. But there is an underground **tunnel** that connects the building to the school, so children don't need to go outside when the weather is bad.

The main way to get to the town is through another tunnel which goes through a mountain. It's quite small and cars can only go one way. The direction changes every 30 minutes.

There's something nice about living close to so many people. But it's important to have good neighbours!

Writing

1 Read Stephen's email to Ricardo. Why is he writing?

Hi Ricardo,

Thanks for your email. It's great that you're coming to visit from Brazil with work next month. We'd love you to come and visit. Our town isn't very famous, so it's a good idea for me to tell you a little bit about it.

I live in a small town called Tring. It's about 30 minutes from London, in beautiful countryside. A lot of people live here and work in London in the week.

It has everything you need: there's a post office, shops and there is even a small theatre! There's a big supermarket just outside town and we go shopping there on Saturday to buy food for the week. There isn't a big cinema, but there's a place where local people watch films outside in the summer. There are some nice cafés and restaurants in the town. People go to the restaurants with their families on Friday night and at the weekend. In the High Street there are some interesting shops and people come to Tring at the weekend to look around them.

There aren't any big parks, but there are three football clubs and a lot of other small sports clubs.

I like my home town. It's a small town, but it's a lovely place. I hope you like it, too.

Call me soon and we can arrange the details for your trip.

All the best
Stephen

2 Read the email again. Are the statements true (T) or false (F)?

1 Tring isn't a big city. ....
2 Most people live and work there. ....
3 There isn't a cinema in Tring. ....
4 There are a lot of places to eat. ....
5 People visit Tring for the shops. ....
6 There's a big park. ....

3 Read the Focus box. Then read the text again and find three more examples of:

1 subject + verb + object   2 adjective + noun

Using word order correctly

Basic word order is:
Subject + verb + object
I   like   my home town.

Adjectives come before nouns.
a small town   NOT   ~~a town small~~
beautiful countryside   NOT   ~~countryside beautiful~~
The usual word order in long sentences is:
People go   to the restaurants with their families
who? + what? + where?   + who with? +
at the weekend.
when?

4 Put the words in the correct order to make sentences.

1 don't like / my city / I / .
   I don't like my city. ....
2 live and work / People / there / .
   ....
3 great / There / some / shops / are / .
   ....
4 have lunch / in summer / in the park / People / .
   ....
5 every day / I / with my friends / go to school / .
   ....
6 with his brother / Jamie / after school / plays football / .
   ....

Prepare

5a Imagine a friend/colleague is visiting you from another country and wants to know about the town or city where you live. Write a reply with a description of your home town or city. First, make notes on what you'll write about. Use the ideas below to help you.
• where it is
• small or big town/city
• who lives there
• places and buildings there
• things people do at the weekend
• who visits the town/city and why

b Decide on the order of the information for your reply.

Write

6 Write your reply. Use your notes in Exercise 5 and the Focus box to help you. Use the email beginning below.
Hi, Stefan,
Thanks for your email. It's great that you're coming to visit me next month. Here's some information about my town.

Vocabulary

Appearance

1 Cross out the alternative that is not correct.

1 She's got *blonde/dark/old/short* hair.
2 He's got *short/blue/brown* eyes.
3 He's quite a *tall/young/long* man.
4 My wife's got *long/black/thin/short* hair.
5 Your brother is quite a *tall/thin/grey* man.
6 You've got beautiful *tall/brown/blue* eyes.

2 Choose the correct alternatives.

1 My sister has long blonde *hair/eyes*.
2 I'm quite *tall/long* and wear glasses.
3 He's got a really *tall/big* nose!
4 Carla is tall and *thin/short*.
5 He's got short hair and *blonde/brown* eyes.
6 James has got amazing *thin/blue* eyes.
7 She's got *tall/long* dark hair.
8 My mum looks *young/old*, but she's 62.

3 Complete the conversations with the missing words.

1 **A:** What does your brother look _____?
   B: He's good-_____. He's tall and he's got blue eyes.
2 **A:** Has your sister got short _____?
   B: No, she hasn't. It's _____ .
3 **A:** Is your mum _____?
   B: No, she isn't. She's quite short.
4 **A:** What _____ your parents look like?
   B: They're quite tall and they both have blue _____ .
5 **A:** How _____ is your friend?
   B: About 195 cm. He's also quite _____-looking.

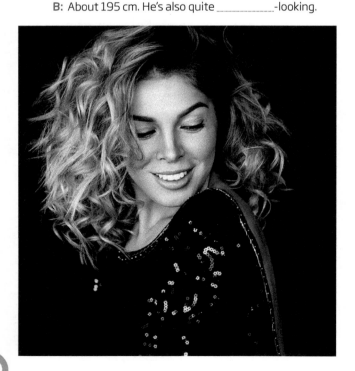

Grammar

Position of adjectives

4 Put the words in the correct order to make sentences.

1 are / You / beautiful / .
   You are beautiful.
2 tall / very / He's / boy / a / .
   ....
3 got long, / hair / She's / dark / .
   ....
4 Andrew's / and thin / tall / .
   ....
5 and fat / My / dad's / short / .
   ....
6 old / She's / nice, / lady / a / .
   ....
7 big, / has / blue eyes / Alice / got / .
   ....
8 a / He's / face / thin / got / .
   ....
9 woman / a / tall / very / Julia's / .
   ....
10 boss / hair / My / has / short, / got / blonde / .
   ....

5 Correct the mistake in each sentence.

   beautiful woman
1 She's a ~~woman beautiful~~.

2 Mike looks like tired today.

3 Janice has got blue, beautiful eyes.

4 My brother's a man very tall.

5 She's got long, hair blonde.

6 My dad's a man tall.

7 What does he looks like?

8 My neighbour is thin and tall.

9 He's got really hair long.

10 He's a man very good-looking.

Vocabulary

Adjectives to describe experiences

1 **Put the letters in the correct order to make adjectives.**
1 fawlu _awful_
2 freptec ....
3 loco ....
4 regta ....
5 ribrohle ....
6 cein ....
7 rongib ....
8 gritnestine ....
9 ritlebre ....
10 voleyl ....

2 **Complete the table with the adjectives in Exercise 1.**

Positive	Negative
	awful

3 **Choose the correct alternatives.**
1 That movie was _boring/cool_. Nothing happened until the end!
2 This meal is _horrible/lovely_. I definitely want to eat here again.
3 It's _OK/great_ – not amzing, but not bad either.
4 Our holiday was _awful/brilliant_. We had an amazing time!
5 This book is really _interesting/terrible_. You should read it.
6 There were lots of _boring/cool_ people at the party. It was great.
7 Can we watch something else? This programme isn't very _interesting/boring_.
8 Oh, this food is _amazing/terrible_! I can't eat it.

Grammar

was/were

4 **Choose the correct alternatives.**
1 My parents _was/were_ very kind to us.
2 _Was/Were_ you hard-working at school?
3 That book _was/were_ very interesting.
4 The lesson _wasn't/weren't_ boring at all.
5 I _was/were_ very happy at school.
6 Wow, they _wasn't/weren't_ very friendly!
7 Emilia _wasn't/weren't_ very polite in the meeting.
8 Alicia _wasn't/weren't_ here yesterday.
9 You _was/were_ very kind to me last week.
10 What _was/were_ your favourite game when you _was/were_ a child?

5 **Complete the text with _was(n't)_ or _were(n't)_.**

> I loved school – it **1** .... great! My teachers **2** .... really kind and the other students **3** .... friendly. There **4** .... a lot of work to do and the lessons **5** .... boring because the teachers **6** .... interesting and funny, too. I miss my school days – they **7** .... fantastic!

6 **Use the prompts and the correct form of _be_ to write sentences and questions.**
1 I / quiet when I / a child.
....
2 Who / your best friend / at school?
....
3 My flatmates / not / at home last week.
....
4 your teachers funny?
....
5 she good / at school?
....
6 your hair blonde / when you / a child?
....
7 He / not / very friendly yesterday.
....
8 Where / you / last night?
....

5c

Grammar
can/can't for ability

1 **Correct the mistake in each sentence.**

1 He can ~~to~~ speak five languages.

2 She cans play the guitar.

3 Do you can count to ten in German?

4 I can't climbing that tree.

5 We can all to speak English.

6 They can't cooking.

7 Play chess you can?

8 I can't to swim very well.

2 **Complete the conversations with *can* or *can't*.**

1 **A:** _____ you swim?
   B: No, I _____ . But I'd like to!

2 **A:** Where are you? I _____ see you.
   B: I'm over here. _____ you see me now?

3 **A:** _____ Carla speak French?
   B: Yes, she _____ . Very well.

4 **A:** _____ you help me?
   B: I'm sorry, I _____ . I have to leave right now.

5 **A:** I _____ climb that tree.
   B: No you _____ !

3 **Use the information to write sentences.**

1 James: play the piano ✓ play the guitar ✗
   James can play the piano, but he can't play the guitar.

2 Anna: make bread ✗ make a good carrot cake ✓

3 I: speak English ✓ speak French ✗

4 My dad: sing quite well ✓ dance ✗

5 Max: fix a car ✗ drive one! ✓

6 I: say some words in Japanese ✓ have a conversation ✗

7 She: play an instrument ✗ sing beautifully ✓

Vocabulary
Skills

4 **Match verbs 1–10 with a–j to make phrases.**

1 count _____
2 drive _____
3 play _____
4 bake _____
5 speak _____
6 climb _____
7 fix _____
8 spell _____
9 run _____
10 make _____

a the word *Caribbean*
b to 50 in Spanish
c another language
d a tree
e pizza
f five kilometres
g the piano
h a car
i a cake
j a computer

5 **Choose the correct alternatives.**

1 Can you *speak/tell* Italian?
2 I think I can *make/fix* your computer for you.
3 Sarah wants to *bake/cook* a meal for us tonight.
4 Would you like to *make/play* chess with me?
5 I can *count/speak* to ten in Korean.
6 I can *run/climb* for five kilometres.
7 Can you *speak/spell* your name for me, please?
8 I want to *bake/cook* a cake for mum's birthday.

6 **Complete the sentences with the missing verbs.**

1 The mechanic says she can't _____ the car.
2 Can you _____ chess?
3 How do you _____ your name?
4 Do you _____ French?
5 Let's _____ a cake for our anniversary.
6 He can _____ really fast.
7 My two-year-old can _____ to ten!
8 Susan can _____ the piano.

Functional language

Make and respond to requests

1 **Match requests 1–8 with responses a–h.**

1 Can I borrow your charger? ....
2 Could you help me clean the house, please? ....
3 Excuse me, could you move your bag, please? ....
4 Can you lend me a pen? ....
5 Could I borrow £5? ....
6 Can you help me with my homework? ....
7 Could you lend me your bike? ....
8 Can you help me fix my computer? ....

a I'm afraid not. I've only got this one.
b I'm sorry, I need it for my phone.
c I can't, I'm sorry. I'm really bad with technology.
d Of course I can. I'm good at maths.
e Sure, no problem. Where are you going?
f Sure, no problem. I'll clean the kitchen.
g I'm afraid not. I haven't got any money myself!
h Of course I can. Sorry, I'll put it up here.

2 **Put the words in the correct order to complete the conversations.**

1 A: the / Can / window / open / you / ?

....

B: Sure, no problem.

2 A: phone / your / Can / borrow / I / ?

....

B: I'm sorry, I need it. I'm waiting for an important call.

3 A: the / Could / me / door / for / open / you / ?

....

B: Of course I can.

4 A: washing-up / me / the / Could / help / you / with / ?

....

B: I can't, I'm sorry. I'm just going out.

5 A: I / here / sit / Can / ?

....

B: Of course you can.

6 A: something / me / with / help / Can / you / ?

....

B: What's that?
A: laptop / office / my / you / get / my / from / Can / ?

....

B: Sure, no problem.

Listening

1 🔊 **5.01** **Listen to two friends, Kim and Harry, discussing some old school photos. How many people do they discuss?**

2 **Listen again and complete the sentences.**

1 Harry's hair was long and ....
2 Harry thinks Kim was .... at school.
3 Kim says she was .... at school.
4 Harry thinks she was .... at school.
5 Luisa wasn't .... to Harry at school.
6 Kim says that Luisa is very .... now.
7 Shaun's hair was .... and blonde.
8 Kim says Shaun had beautiful .... eyes.

3a **Are the sentences true (T) or false (F)?**

1 Kim thinks Harry's hair was funny at school. ....
2 Kim wants to show Harry her school photo. ....
3 Harry thinks Kim isn't good-looking now. ....
4 Harry thinks Kim isn't quiet now. ....
5 Harry likes the fashion from when they were at school. ....
6 He thinks Luisa didn't like him at school. ....
7 Kim says Luisa is different now. ....
8 She says Luisa has a boring job now. ....

b **Listen again and check.**

4 **Match the words/phrases in bold 1–3 with meanings a–c.**

1 Oh Harry, look at that **hairstyle**! ....
2 I know. **Moving** quickly **on** ... .
3 She always **called me names**. ....

a starting something new
b use unkind words about someone
c the way you do your hair

Reading

1 Read the social media post. Complete the replies 1–4 with sentences a–d.

a Prepare some questions.

b Be polite!

c Think of real examples.

d Tell the truth.

2 Read the post again and answer the questions.

Which person …

a thinks it's difficult to talk about something that isn't true?

b gives ideas about what to ask?

c thinks you shouldn't speak too much?

d says you need to prepare some questions for the interview?

e says it's important to talk about your experience?

f says it's important to be nice?

g describes something that happened in an interview?

3 Read the post again. Are the sentences true (T) or false (F)?

1 It's important to listen to what the interviewer is asking. ....

2 You can show that you are friendly by smiling and being polite. ....

3 You should always say you've got good qualifications. ....

4 It's a good idea to think of questions after the interview. ....

5 You should ask about things you want to know about the interviewer's life. ....

6 You should use positive adjectives to describe yourself. ....

4 Find words or phrases in the replies with meanings 1–5.

1 conversation about things like the weather (2 words, *Jane Harper*)

2 certifications you get from school or university (*Gavin Fields*)

3 information about something (*Gavin Fields*)

4 usual/normal (*Catherine Williams*)

5 good (*Joe Mattis*)

Michael Dennis | 1 hr

Hi, everyone. I've got a job interview next week. What can I do to prepare? Thanks!

4 Replies

Jane Harper | 53 mins

1 .... Make small talk, but don't talk too much. Listen carefully to the questions. Remember to say thank you for the interview and smile and be friendly. Show them that you're a nice person to work with.

Gavin Fields | 48 mins

2 .... In my last interview I was very nervous and I lied about my qualifications. They knew it wasn't true because I wasn't sure about my answers and I didn't give many details.

Catherine Williams | 41 mins

3 .... Think of things you want to know about the job a few days before the interview and write them down. If you ask questions, this shows that you're really interested in the job. Good questions to ask are: *What does a typical day look like?* or *What do you like about working for this company?*

Joe Mattis | 32 mins

4 .... Don't just say 'I'm hard-working', think of things you can say to show it, for example, 'I always finish my work before I go home.' Think of a few different examples which show positive things about you so you can answer their questions quickly.

Writing

1 Read the notice for a TV talent show. What information do they want?

   a a short video

   b a short description

   c some photos

SHOW US YOUR SKILLS AND BE ON TV!

Send us your applications for the new TV programme

So you think you've got skills?

Write and tell us in 150 words who you are and what your special skill is. We'll ask the best applicants to come on the show.

2 Read Tia's application and answer the questions.

   1 What's her special skill?

   2 What does she want to do on the show?

1 My name's Tia and I was born in India in 1998. My parents are English, but they were there for work. They were very kind to me when I was a child and I was always happy.

2 I've got short dark hair and brown eyes. I'm tall and thin. I think I'm very friendly. I was quiet when I was a child, but I'm not now. My friends think I talk a lot!

3 My special skill is that I can speak EIGHT languages including Hindi, Gujarati, English, French and many more. I think I've got skills because I can also sing in each language. On the show I want to sing a song using each language I know. Please choose me!

3 Read the Focus box. Then match the paragraph descriptions in the box with the paragraphs in Tia's application.

Using paragraphs

Use paragraphs to organise what you write into different topics. This makes it easier for the reader to follow your ideas. For example, in Exercise 2, Tia writes about three topics:

- her special skill   _____
- her background/childhood   _____
- a description of her now   _____

4 Read Justin's application. Mark the start of paragraphs two and three with /.

My name's Justin and I was born in San Francisco in the US. My parents were artists and they loved painting pictures all the time. My earliest memory was being in their studio, painting pictures with my hands. It was very funny! I'm a bit quiet, but I'm always kind and I try to be friendly. I'm quite tall and I'm not fat, but I'm not thin, I'm medium. I've got short blonde hair and blue eyes. My special skill is that I can paint – really fast! On the show I want to paint a picture in under two minutes. I think you'll be surprised that I can paint a good picture in just two minutes, and the people watching will love it. Please choose me!

Prepare

5 You're going to write an application to go on the TV programme. First, make notes about these things:

- your background/childhood
- a description of you (appearance and personality)
- your special skill (it can be real or invent one)
- what you'd like to do on the show
- why you think it's good for TV

Write

6 Write your application. Use your notes in Exercise 5 and the Focus box to help you.

Vocabulary

Prepositions

1 Choose the correct option, a, b or c.

1 Leave your dirty shoes _____ the room, please.
   a at   b in   c outside

2 Where were you _____ Saturday?
   a on   b in   c at

3 I'll meet you _____ the entrance.
   a on   b at   c in

4 The bus station is _____ the castle, on the right.
   a next to   b on   c inside

5 You can buy food _____ the food tent.
   a on   b near   c in

6 Is there a car park _____ here?
   a at   b on   c near

7 Do you study _____ the morning?
   a in   b at   c on

8 Why are all your books _____ the floor?
   a at   b on   c outside

9 I usually wake up _____ 6 a.m.
   a on   b in   c at

10 There are a lot of shops _____ my house.
   a on   b inside   c near

2 Correct the mistake in each sentence.

                 in
1 Reena's café is ~~on~~ the city centre.

2 I watched a film next to my friend's house last night.

3 The children are inside, playing in the garden.

4 The shop's closed in Mondays.

5 The sports centre is next of the stadium.

6 My brother lives inside London.

7 Is there a post office next to here?

8 What do you usually do in the weekend?

Grammar

Past simple (regular verbs)

3 Choose the correct alternatives.

1 I *studied/studed* all evening on Thursday.

2 I *didn't/don't* like apples when I was a child.

3 We *watched/watch* a good film last weekend.

4 She *doesn't/didn't* call me yesterday.

5 I *finish/finished* work early last Friday.

6 I *didn't study/didn't studied* English when I was a child.

7 Sorry I'm late, I *missed/miss* the bus this morning.

8 I *cried/cryed* when she told me.

4 Complete the sentences with the past simple form of the verbs in brackets.

1 I ___*played*___ (play) football with my friends last weekend.

2 Rosa _____ (want) to be a doctor when she was a child.

3 I _____ (not dance) at the party.

4 My dad _____ (cook) dinner for me yesterday.

5 They _____ (not invite) us to their party.

6 We _____ (paint) our kitchen last week.

7 I _____ (live) near the sea when I was a child.

8 He _____ (not listen) to classical music when he was a teenager.

9 We _____ (talk) for hours last night.

10 I _____ (not study) much for the exam.

5 Complete the text with the past simple form of the verbs in the box.

be   call   cook   invite   laugh   play   study   talk
try   watch

Last weekend ¹_____ great! My friend ²_____ me on Saturday morning and ³_____ me to his house for dinner. He ⁴_____ a really nice meal and I ⁵_____ a new kind of chocolate dessert – yum! We ⁶_____ about our studies for a long time then we ⁷_____ some comedy on TV. It was really funny and I ⁸_____ a lot. I ⁹_____ on Sunday morning because I have a test this week. In the afternoon, I ¹⁰_____ tennis with my sister and I won!

Vocabulary

Irregular verbs

1 Match infinitives 1–12 with past simple forms a–l.

1	take	a	went
2	wake up	b	took
3	throw	c	sat
4	drive	d	threw
5	go	e	bought
6	buy	f	brought
7	feel	g	saw
8	leave	h	caught
9	see	i	drove
10	catch	j	left
11	sit	k	woke up
12	bring	l	felt

2 Complete the text with the past simple form of the verbs in the box.

buy   drive   feel   go   leave   see   sit
wake up

Last summer I **1**_____ on a trip with a group of friends. I **2**_____ a new car and we **3**_____ it to the beach. It was a long journey, but we **4**_____ early and arrived there at lunchtime. Then we **5**_____ on the beach all afternoon. I **6**_____ tired, so I slept a while. When I **7**_____ , I **8**_____ my friends in the sea, so I joined them. Finally, we went home late. We had a great time.

3 Choose the correct alternatives.

1 I *fell/felt* sad this morning, but I'm OK now.
2 She *sat/saw* down next to me.
3 I *brought/bought* a new phone from the shop last week.
4 Kara *left/went* the party early.
5 We *brought/bought* our own lunch from home today.
6 Last month they *saw/went* to the Natural History Museum.
7 Mike *drove/took* to work this morning.
8 I *did/made* you a cake for your birthday.

Grammar

Past simple (irregular verbs)

4 Choose the correct option, a or b.

1	He _____ the ball to me.	a	throw	b	threw
2	I _____ my laptop to school yesterday.	a	took	b	taked
3	I _____ the ball!	a	caught	b	catched
4	We _____ Maria at the party last night.	a	didn't saw	b	didn't see
5	They _____ work early last Thursday.	a	left	b	leaved
6	I _____ well last week.	a	didn't fell	b	didn't feel
7	Mark _____ his daughter to work yesterday.	a	bought	b	brought
8	We _____ to Italy for our last holiday.	a	drove	b	drive

5 Complete the sentences with the past simple form of the verbs in brackets.

1 I _____ (have) breakfast early this morning.
2 I was late, so I _____ (miss) the bus this morning.
3 I _____ (bring) you a cup of coffee.
4 Yesterday Sally _____ (feel) ill, so she _____ (not go) to work.
5 I _____ (buy) a new laptop yesterday.
6 I'm tired – I _____ (wake up) really early this morning.
7 She _____ (drive) to Edinburgh at the weekend.
8 Mark _____ (not see) his friends last week.
9 We _____ (go) to the cinema last night.
10 My girlfriend _____ (make) me a beautiful cake for my birthday.

6 Use the diary to write sentences about Maya's week last week.

Monday	**1**Catch a train to London ✓
	2~~Lunch with Sam~~ move to next week
Tuesday	**3**Give a presentation ✓
	4Have dinner with Jenny ✓
Wednesday	**5**~~Phone Lucas~~ busy – phone on Monday
	6~~Drive to Manchester~~ take train instead
Thursday	**7**Buy a new watch ✓
	8Go to the theatre ✗
Friday	**9**~~Gym?~~ too tired!
	10Meet Carla ✓

1 *She caught a train to London.*
2 *She didn't have lunch with Sam.*
3 _____
4 _____
5 _____
6 _____
7 _____
8 _____
9 _____
10 _____

6c

Vocabulary

Verbs + prepositions

1 Choose the correct alternatives.

1 Who do you live *with/by*?
2 I met up *for/with* my friends last night.
3 We moved *to/for* this house last year.
4 I need to talk *for/to* Andrew as soon as possible.
5 My wife works *as/to* a teacher.
6 Let's walk *to/for* the café, it's not far.
7 I usually listen *at/to* a podcast on the bus.
8 Come and dance *with/from* us!
9 He travelled *to/for* all seven continents last year.
10 I went *in/to* Cambridge on Saturday.

2 Complete the sentences with a preposition.

1 We met up _____ our friends from school last weekend.
2 Dan travelled _____ the island by boat.
3 When I was a student, I worked _____ a shop assistant.
4 My parents moved _____ a new house last year.
5 I always listen _____ music in the car.
6 I walked _____ school every day when I was a child.
7 I live _____ my parents.
8 What university do you go _____ ?
9 I danced _____ her at the wedding.
10 Yes, I talked _____ him about it yesterday.

3 Use the prompts to write sentences and questions.

1 When / you / listen / music?
    When do you listen to music?
2 I walk / work every day.
    ....
3 Who / you / talk / at / party last weekend?
    ....
4 Colin worked / bus driver / he was younger.
    ....
5 Sally went / a girls' school / she was a child.
    ....
6 They travelled / Italy by bus.
    ....
7 I meet up / my friends once / week.
    ....
8 They listen / the news / the radio every morning.
    ....
9 She live / her sister / New York.
    ....
10 I moved / France / I was 10.
    ....

Grammar

Past simple (questions)

4 Complete the conversations with the missing words.

1 A: Where _____ you go to school?
   B: In London.
2 A: _____ you go to the cinema last night?
   B: Yes, I _____ .
   A: _____ did you go with?
   B: My sister.
3 A: _____ she talk to you this morning?
   B: No, she _____ .
4 A: _____ they have a good time last night?
   B: I don't know. Why? Where _____ they go?
5 A: How _____ you travel to France?
   B: By train.
6 A: _____ you study for the exam?
   B: Yes, I _____ . All weekend!
   A: _____ did you study?
   B: Geography.

5 Put the words in the correct order to make questions.

1 a / night / Did / film / watch / you / last / ?
   ....
2 to / did / university / go / Where / you / ?
   ....
3 your / you / school / like / Did / ?
   ....
4 Who / night / meet up with / did / you / last / ?
   ....
5 walk / Why / work / to / they / did / ?
   ....
6 weekend / What / do / did / last / you / ?
   ....
7 time / good / Did / a / you / have / ?
   ....
8 to Adriana / did / talk / you / When / ?
   ....

6 Write questions for the answers.

1 *Did you have a good time on holiday?*
   Yes, we had a good time on holiday.
2 ....
   I went to school in South East London.
3 ....
   No, I didn't play video games when I was a child.
4 ....
   They left early because it was boring.
5 ....
   Yes, I talked to David last night.
6 ....
   Yes, they moved to a big house.

Functional language
Give and accept an apology

1 Match the sentence halves.

1 I'm really ....
2 No ....
3 That's all ....
4 That's ....
5 I'm sorry I'm ....
6 I'm afraid ....

a right.
b fine.
c sorry.
d problem.
e late.
f I didn't talk to Marjorie.

2 Which of the sentences in Exercise 1 are ways of saying sorry (S)? Which are ways of responding to apologies (R)?

1 ....   3 ....   5 ....
2 ....   4 ....   6 ....

3 Choose the correct alternatives.

1 **A:** Excuse me, can I get past?
  B: Oh, *sorry/afraid.*
  A: No *fine/worries.*

2 **A:** I'm *really/afraid* I can't come to work today, I don't feel well.
  B: *That's/That* fine. I hope you feel better soon.

3 **A:** Can I borrow your phone charger?
  B: *I'm/I* sorry, I need it myself.
  A: That's *all/OK* right.

4 **A:** I'm *sorry/afraid* we're late. There was a lot of traffic this morning.
  B: That's *OK/worries.* Come in.

5 **A:** Ouch! That's my foot!
  B: Oh no! I'm *so/too* sorry! I didn't see you.

6 **A:** I'm *afraid/worries* I didn't do the homework.
  B: *No/None* problem, I know you're busy. Can you do it for tomorrow?

7 **A:** Would you like to come to my party on Saturday?
  B: *I'm/I* afraid I can't. I've got other plans.
  A: No *worries/fine.* Next time, maybe?

8 **A:** Did you break this glass?
  B: Yes, I did. I'm *badly/really* sorry.
  A: That's *right/OK.* We've got more.

Listening

1 🔊 **6.01** Listen to Rachel and Connor talking about an experience she had and answer the questions.

1 'Glamping' is …
  a camping in a city.
  b very comfortable camping.
  c staying in a hotel.

2 Did Rachel enjoy the experience?

2 Listen again and put Connor's questions in the order he asks them.

a Did you cook? ....
b What did you do the next day? ....
c Did you like it? ....
d When did you leave? ....
e What did you do? ....
f Why was that? ....
g What did you eat? ....

3a Match Rachel's answers 1–7 with Connor's questions a–g in Exercise 2.

1 The furniture was comfortable and there were a lot of things in the 'tent'. ....
2 Yes ....
3 No ....
4 We had breakfast then went for a long walk. ....
5 chicken and pasta ....
6 at midday ....
7 We arrived there in the afternoon and saw our 'tent'. ....

b Listen again and check.

4 Match the words in bold 1–4 with meanings a–d.

1 … staying in a **tent** in the countryside. ....
2 What about a glamping **experience**? ....
3 And it was **luxury**. ....
4 … then we **ate out** in town. ....

a have dinner in a restaurant
b something that you do that you remember
c a place to sleep, made of material
d very high quality and very comfortable

Reading

1 Read the article about gift experiences. Complete it with headings a–d.

a Try a new hobby

b A weekend away

c Adventure!

d Try a new sport

2 Read the article again. Choose the correct alternatives.

1 It can be *expensive*/*difficult* to buy presents for some people.

2 'Gift experiences' are *activities*/*objects*.

3 Trying a new sport is a *good*/*bad* way to do exercise.

4 You can try a new sport with a special *class*/*person*.

5 There are *a few*/*a lot of* different types of hobbies to try.

6 You can learn a *new*/*difficult* skill.

7 A weekend away is good for someone who *needs to relax*/*likes to travel*.

8 Adventure gifts are *safe*/*dangerous*.

3 Read the article again and answer the questions.

1 Why are some people difficult to buy presents for? (two reasons)

2 When do you pay for the activity: *before* or *after* the person does it?

3 What are the advantages of trying a new sport? (two advantages)

4 What two examples of trying a new hobby does the text give?

5 What might the person discover when they learn a new hobby?

6 What's the extra advantage of buying someone a weekend away?

7 What three examples of adventure gifts does the text give?

8 What kind of people would like an adventure gift?

4 Match the words in bold in the article with meanings 1–4.

1 something very exciting ....

2 the first one ....

3 very good ....

4 a short holiday ....

A different type of gift

Sometimes it's difficult to buy presents for people on their birthday. Maybe they've got everything they want, or maybe they haven't got any hobbies or interests. In this case *something to do* (not *something to have*) can be a good idea. 'Gift experiences' are popular at the moment.

You buy a 'ticket' which the person can then use for a class or activity. We look at four of the best types.

1 ....

This is a **fantastic** way to do exercise and have fun at the same time. There are lots of wonderful and interesting things to try, from playing tennis to swimming. Most places offer an **introductory** session as a present for someone to try for the first time.

2 ....

For example, you could buy your special person an online guitar course or a sushi-making class. There are hundreds of different ideas out there. It's an awesome way to learn a new skill and discover something new.

3 ....

Does your special person work a lot? Do they need a **break** and some time to relax? Nowadays it's easy to travel to different places quite quickly. So why not buy them a mini-holiday? (You can enjoy it too!)

4 ....

These are really exciting. Examples include a flying lesson, driving fast cars and 'survival' experiences. This type of present is great for people who want something exciting or a **thrill**. They might look dangerous, but they're all very safe.

Writing

1 Look at the social media post and read Shahla's comment. Which country were they in?

Claire Dunlop
September 24

Vicky Morgan Hannah Richards
Shahla James, remember this? One year ago today!

Shahla James | 8 mins

Oh yes, I remember this! 😃 Was it really a YEAR ago today?!? We had such a good time on that holiday. We travelled to Italy and we stayed in that little hotel. I remember that day clearly. We all woke up at 3 a.m. so we could watch the sunrise at the top of the mountain. Hannah was tired and complained all the way! I think she didn't want to get out of bed, but we made her! The sunrise was so beautiful. Do you remember we drank coffee and talked about our plans for the year? Then we got back to the town and had that beautiful lunch by the river. You had fish and Vicky had that lovely chicken dish. Then we were all tired and slept for the rest of the afternoon!

Vicky Morgan
Good times! ☺

2 Read the social media post again. Put events a–e in the correct order.

a They drank coffee. ....
b They had lunch. ....
c They got up early. ....
d They slept. ....
e Hannah complained. ....

3 Read the Focus box. Then look at Shahla's comment again. Find three more examples of sentences with two clauses where the subject pronoun is not repeated.

Using subject pronouns

Subject pronouns are words like *I, you, he, she, we* and *they*.
A clause is a group of words that includes a subject pronoun and a verb.
We had *such a good time on that holiday*.
Sometimes we connect two clauses with words like *and* and *but*.
We travelled to Italy *and* ***we stayed in that little hotel***.
A clause can only have one subject.
Hannah *was tired* NOT ***Hannah*** ~~*she*~~ *was tired*.
When a sentence has two clauses and the subject is the same, we don't need to repeat the subject pronoun.
Hannah was tired *and* ***complained all the way***!
Both subject pronouns are necessary when the subject in each clause is different.
She *didn't want to get out of bed, but* ***we*** *made her*.
NOT ~~*She didn't want to get out of bed, but made her.*~~

4 Make sentences with *and*. Miss out the second subject pronoun if you can.

1 We had dinner. We talked about our lives.
   We had dinner and talked about our lives.

2 I went to the party. Chris talked to me.

3 My mum came round last night. She cooked dinner.

4 Anita got up early. She had breakfast.

5 Jamie ordered fish. Alice ordered chicken.

6 She looked at me. I smiled at her.

7 Lisa and Charles went out. They watched a film.

8 Charlotte and I went to the museum. We saw a dinosaur.

Prepare

5 You're going to write a social media post about a special memory you have. Follow the instructions below and make notes.

1 Choose a photo you have of an important memory.
2 Make notes on these things:
   • Where were you?
   • Who were you with?
   • What did you do before and after the photo?
   • Why is it a special memory?

Write

6 Write your social media post. Use your notes in Exercise 5 and the Focus box to help you.

7A

Vocabulary
Food and drink

1 Put the letters in the correct order to make words for food and drink.

1 nekihcc   *chicken*
2 fots kirnds _____
3 tame   _____
4 ladsa   _____
5 fecoef   _____
6 rufti   _____
7 snabe   _____
8 ate   _____
9 gesg   _____
10 cujei   _____
11 hisf   _____
12 gaebletsev _____

2 Complete the table with the words in Exercise 1.

from animals	from plants	drinks
chicken		

3 Choose the correct alternatives.

1 After dinner, I usually have a little *fruit/meat* for dessert.
2 I never eat *frozen food/salad*. I only eat fresh things.
3 Diane's a vegetarian, so she doesn't eat any *vegetables/meat*.
4 This orange *juice/coffee* is delicious.
5 Would you like sugar in your *coffee/juice*?
6 Orange juice is my favourite *fruit/soft drink*.
7 Would you like rice or *pasta/chicken* with your fish?
8 Green beans are my favourite *fruit/vegetables*.

Grammar
Countable and uncountable nouns; *some, any, lots of* and *a lot of*

4 Are the nouns in the box countable (C) or uncountable (U)?

> beans   chicken   coffee   eggs   fish
> frozen food   fruit   pasta   rice
> soft drinks   tea   vegetables

5 Choose the correct alternatives.

1 There *is/are* some carrots in the fridge.
2 We *have/haven't* got any milk.
3 Can you buy *some/any* sugar, please?
4 Would you like *a/some* cheese?
5 These eggs *is/are* delicious!
6 *Is/Are* there any rice left?
7 There *isn't/aren't* any salt in it.
8 Have we got *some/any* chocolate?
9 Well, let's get *some/any* food first.
10 Could you get me *a/some* bottle of water?

6 Complete the sentences with one word.

1 _____ there any tomatoes in the fridge?
2 My son's favourite food _____ pizza!
3 I think there's _____ pasta in that cupboard.
4 We haven't got _____ bread left.
5 I'd like _____ chicken sandwich, please.
6 Excuse me, where _____ the frozen food section?
7 No, there aren't _____ eggs in this recipe.
8 Would you like _____ piece of cake?
9 I don't want _____ butter on mine, thanks.
10 I bought _____ oranges at the supermarket.

Grammar

how much/ how many? + quantifiers

1 **Complete the questions with *much* or *many*.**
1 How _____ rice do you eat?
2 How _____ cups of coffee do you drink a day?
3 How _____ milk do we need?
4 How _____ fish have we got?
5 How _____ onions are in this recipe?
6 How _____ pizzas shall we buy for the party?
7 How _____ oil do we need?
8 How _____ juice do you want?

2 **Choose the correct alternatives.**
1 **A:** How *much/many* milk do you want in your coffee?
   B: Just a *few/little*.
2 **A:** How *much/many* eggs have we got?
   B: *None/Any*. Can you buy some?
3 **A:** We need *some/none* onions.
   B: How *much/many* do we need?
4 **A:** How *much/many* sweets are there?
   B: There aren't *some/any*. Sorry!
5 **A:** How *much/many* chocolate is there?
   B: *Lot/Lots*.
6 **A:** How *much/many* bananas do you want?
   B: Just a *few/little*.
7 **A:** How *much/many* meat do you eat?
   B: I'm a vegetarian. I don't eat *none/any* meat.
8 **A:** Would you like *a/some* rice?
   B: Yes, please.
   A: How *much/many*?
   B: Just a *few/little*. Thanks.

3 **Correct the mistake in each sentence.**
   many
1 How ~~much~~ potatoes have you got?

2 We've got lot of cheese.

3 We haven't got none coffee.

4 How many milk do you want in your tea?

5 We've got some bread, but we haven't got a lot rice.

6 Can I have a little of your crisps, please?

7 I don't think there's some orange juice left.

8 We've still got a little tomatoes in the fridge.

Vocabulary

Food containers

4 **Match containers 1–10 with food/drinks a–j. Some food/drinks may go with more than one container.**
   1 carton of _____
   2 tin of _____
   3 bag of _____
   4 cup of _____
   5 bottle of _____
   6 packet of _____
   7 bar of _____
   8 box of _____
   9 can of _____
   10 jar of _____

   a beans   e tea   h pasta
   b chocolate f water   i rice
   c juice   g cola   j coffee
   d eggs

5 **Choose the correct alternatives.**
   1 Can you help me? I can't open this *bag/carton* of orange juice.
   2 Please buy a *cup/jar* of coffee from the supermarket.
   3 Where is the *box/can* of eggs?
   4 We need two *tins/packets* of tomatoes.
   5 Would you like a *can/tin* of cola?
   6 Put a *bottle/box* of water in your bag to take with you.
   7 Let's have a *cup/jar* of tea.
   8 When I was a child, my mum bought me a *packet/bar* of chocolate when I was good.

Vocabulary

Describing places to eat

1 **Put the letters in the clues in the correct order to complete the crossword.**

Across
- 6 crotlembafo
- 8 loco
- 9 rehfs
- 11 drewcod
- 12 rigbht
- 13 dromen
- 14 krad

Down
- 1 ecni
- 2 lethayh
- 3 slaml
- 4 sinoy
- 5 rangset
- 7 pensexvie
- 10 lappour

2 **Complete the sentences with the words in the box.**

crowded	dark	expensive	modern	noisy
popular	small	strange		

1 Sorry, I can't hear you. It's really _____ in here.
2 It's really _____. I spent over £100 last time I went.
3 Why is it so _____? I can't see my food!
4 It's close to the Eiffel Tower, so it's _____ with tourists.
5 This place gets really _____ on a Friday night.
6 The building is old, but it's quite _____ inside.
7 It's a _____ café – there are cat pictures everywhere!
8 There's a _____ garden with a few tables out the back.

Grammar

Comparative adjectives

3 **Complete the sentences with the comparative forms of the adjectives in brackets.**

1 The lights are _____ (bright) in the kitchen.
2 The food is _____ (fresh) than in most places.
3 The coffee here is _____ (expensive), but it tastes amazing!
4 It's a lot _____ (noisy) downstairs I'm afraid.
5 Our new place is _____ (large) than our old one.
6 Your phone is _____ (good) than mine.
7 Sushi is _____ (healthy) than fast food.
8 Pizza is _____ (delicious) than pasta, I think.

4 **Correct the mistake in each sentence.**

        more crowded
1 Tom's Café is always ~~crowdeder~~ than the River Café.

2 Canada is more bigger than France.

3 My lunch is healthyier than yours.

4 This café is much better then the old one.

5 The food here is much expensiver.

6 This car is more small than your old one.

7 It's much niceer than I remember.

8 English food is badder than Italian.

5 **Use the prompts to write comparative sentences.**

1 trains / fast / cars.
   Trains are faster than cars.
2 salad / healthy / burgers.

3 eating out / expensive / eating at home.

4 This film / good / the first one.

5 Tokyo / big / New York.

6 dogs / friendly / cats.

7 Canada / cold / Egypt.

8 sofas / comfortable / chairs.

Functional language
Order in a café

1 Put the words in the correct order to make sentences or questions.

1 sandwich, / I'd / please / this / like / .

....

2 that / with / Any / drinks / hot / ?

....

3 tea, / Can / a / I / large / please / get / ?

....

4 that / How / is / much / ?

....

5 take / in / out / Eat / or / ?

....

2 Choose the correct alternatives.

a Yes, of course. *Take/Sit* a seat and I'll bring it over.

b Yes, please. *I/I'd* like a small cappuccino.

c Eat *in/out*, please.

d Would you *want/like* it hot or cold?

e *Five/A five* pounds twenty, please.

3 Match questions and sentences 1–5 in Exercise 1 with responses a–e in Exercise 2.

1 ....
2 ....
3 ....
4 ....
5 ....

4 Complete the conversation with the missing words.

A: Can I ¹.................... ?

B: I'd ².................... this sandwich, please.

A: Would you like it hot or ³.................... ?

B: Hot, please.

A: Certainly. Any hot drinks with
⁴.................... ?

B: Yes. ⁵.................... I have a small latte, please?

A: A small latte. Of course. Eat in or
⁶.................... out?

B: Eat in, please.

A: OK. Anything ⁷.................... ?

B: No thanks. How ⁸.................... is that?

A: Six pounds seventy, please.

B: Can I ⁹.................... by card?

A: Of course. Take a seat and I'll bring your food ¹⁰.................... .

B: Thank you.

Listening

1 🔊 **7.01 Listen to a radio programme. Which statement is true?**

a Jeff grows all of the food he eats.

b Jeff grows a lot of the food he eats.

c Jeff grows a little of the food he eats.

2 Listen again. Are the sentences true (T) or false (F)?

1 Jeff grows fruit, vegetables and herbs. ....

2 He's a vegetarian. ....

3 He buys a few things to eat. ....

4 He grew potatoes first. ....

5 He didn't like tomatoes at the end of the first year. ....

6 He grows more vegetables every year. ....

7 He grows food because it's cheaper than buying it. ....

8 He throws away a lot of food now. ....

3a Choose the correct option, a or b.

1 He grows herbs .... his house.
   a inside   b outside

2 He eats .... meat.
   a a little   b a lot of

3 Buying food is .... than growing food.
   a cheaper   b more expensive

4 His garden gets .... sunlight.
   a some   b a lot of

5 In the first year, he had .... tomatoes.
   a a few   b a lot of

6 He likes the fact that he .... his own food.
   a cared for   b worked hard for

b Listen again and check.

4 Match the words in bold in extracts 1–4 with meanings a–d.

1 I grow **herbs** in the kitchen, too. ....

2 I think I make **the majority** of what I eat. ....

3 So I decided to **plant** some tomatoes. ....

4 ... so that you don't **waste** or throw away food. ....

a put plants in the ground to grow

b a small plant used to improve the taste of food

c use in a bad way

d most

43

Reading

1 Read the introduction to a recipe book. Who is it for?

  a people who want to cook something new

  b people who don't know how to cook

  c people who don't have a lot of time

2 Read the introduction again. Match paragraphs 1–5 with headings a–e.

  a Why learn? ....

  b Using recipes ....

  c The things you need ....

  d Try new ideas ....

  e Some basic ingredients ....

3 Read the introduction again. Are the statements true (T) or false (F)?

  1 Cooking is difficult. ....

  2 You need to buy good knives. ....

  3 You don't need to buy everything at first. ....

  4 Only use the recipes in the book. ....

  5 Remember to follow the recipes when you start learning to cook. ....

  6 Some ingredients mix well with other ingredients. ....

  7 It's best to cook alone. ....

4 Find words 1–5 in the introduction and match them with meanings a–e.

  1 ingredients (paragraph 1) ....

  2 set (paragraph 2) ....

  3 recipe (paragraph 4) ....

  4 amount (paragraph 4) ....

  5 experiment (paragraph 5) ....

  a instructions telling you how to make a dish

  b try new things

  c the number of things

  d the kinds of food you use to make a dish

  e a group of things which are similar

1 Nowadays, it's easy to buy our meals quickly and cheaply. We don't need to spend hours in the kitchen preparing meals. So why cook? Cooking your own meals is easier than you think. It's also fun and interesting. As you learn about different ingredients and ways of cooking, your meals become more delicious. So how do you start?

2 First of all, you need a few knives. These are important, so make sure you buy a good set. You also need things to cook with and a good oven. Don't buy a lot of things at first. Keep it simple and just buy what you need.

3 There are a few basic things you need for every recipe: salt, pepper and oil. You might need a few other things, but don't buy everything at first. Over time, buy what you need for every recipe you use.

4 Only choose a few simple recipes to start with. You can find a lot of simple recipes in this book, but you can also look on the internet. There are a lot of free recipes there. When you start cooking, follow the recipes exactly. Use exactly the amounts the recipes say to use and cook things for exactly the amount of time the recipes say. Try to remember what things go well with other things. For example, parmesan cheese often goes well with lemon.

5 Don't be afraid to try new things as you learn more about cooking. You can change recipes that you cooked before, or you can experiment with different kinds of food. You can also create a recipe of your own. Share your ideas online or with friends and ask other people to share their ideas with you. Cooking is a great way to make friends and enjoy your food together!

4

Writing

1 Read the review of a place to eat. Did the writer like it?

Guillermo's Mexican Street Food

 Reviewed 25 September

We ate here last night after we went to the cinema. We thought it was brilliant because the food is real Mexican street food (Guillermo is Mexican). I had the vegetable tacos and my boyfriend had a chicken burrito. I think the food is delicious because it's all fresh.

It's also cheap because it's a food truck, not a restaurant. However, there are tables and comfortable chairs outside. It has a nice atmosphere because Guillermo and the people who work with him are very friendly.

It gets crowded later in the evening because the food truck is very popular in the local area. So it's a good idea to arrive early.

I really like this place because it's cheap, comfortable and the food is delicious!

2 Read the review again and answer the questions.
1 Why did the writer think it was brilliant?
....
2 What did they eat?
....
3 Why is it cheap?
....
4 Why does it have a nice atmosphere?
....
5 Why does it get crowded later?
....
6 What two adjectives does the writer use to describe the place in the last line?
....

3 Read the Focus box. Then find four more opinions and reasons in the review.

Giving opinions and reasons

To give opinions, you can use the phrases *I think* and *I don't think* to introduce your ideas.
I think *that new film is great.*
When you talk about past experiences, use *thought/didn't think*.
We **thought** *the story was brilliant.*
You can also give opinions using positive adjectives like *amazing, delicious, exciting, good, interesting* or *lovely* and negative adjectives like *awful, bad, boring* or *horrible.*
The ice cream was **delicious***.*
Use *because* to give a reason for the opinion.
The place isn't good **because** *it's always crowded.*

4 Match opinions 1–6 with reasons a–f.
1 The food is expensive ....
2 I think the restaurant is cool ....
3 I thought the film was boring ....
4 I don't like that café ....
5 I love this sofa ....
6 The menu is fantastic ....

a because it's popular and modern.
b because it's very good quality.
c because there are so many interesting dishes.
d because it's always too crowded.
e because the story wasn't interesting.
f because it's very comfortable.

Prepare

5 You're going to write a review of a place to eat. First choose a place and make notes about these things:
* why you (don't) like it
* what food they sell
* the price (cheap or expensive) and why
* advice for eating there

Write

6 Write your review. Use your notes in Exercise 5 and the Focus box to help you.

8A

Vocabulary
Geography

1 **Put the letters in the correct order to make words.**
1 stoudeciryn *countryside*
2 kys ....
3 rai ....
4 veirr ....
5 ase ....
6 seert ....
7 habec ....
8 trawe ....
9 ladsin ....
10 antonumi ....

2 **Choose the correct option, a, b or c.**
1 We walked for six hours to the top of the ....
   a island   b beach   c mountain
2 The .... went dark and it started to rain.
   a sky   b beach   c river
3 There's .... in the middle of the river.
   a a mountain   b an island   c a sea
4 I usually just lie on the .... all day on holiday.
   a beach   b river   c sea
5 I grew up in the ...., but now I live in a big city.
   a countryside   b sea   c trees
6 The .... is clean in the countryside.
   a river   b beach   c air
7 Plastic in the .... is a big problem nowadays.
   a air   b sea   c mountain
8 You can't drink the .... from the sea.
   a water   b beach   c river
9 The .... runs through the city.
   a sea   b river   c air
10 There are lots of tall .... by the side of the road.
   a trees   b beaches   c islands

3 **Complete the sentences with words in Exercises 1 and 2.**
1 Be careful in the sea, the .... is very cold!
2 We took a boat trip down the ....
3 I live near the sea, so in the summer we always go to the ....
4 The night .... was full of stars.
5 Do you live in the .... or in a city?
6 Ben Nevis is the highest .... in the UK.
7 I went outside to get some fresh ....
8 Hawaii is an .... in the North Pacific Ocean.
9 There are over 390 billion .... in the Amazon rainforest.
10 I don't like swimming in the .... – I'm scared of sharks!

Grammar
Present continuous

4 **Use the prompts to write sentences or questions with the present continuous.**
1 I / have / dinner.
   I'm having dinner.
2 Gillian / play / football / at / moment.
   ....
3 My parents / not work / today.
   ....
4 What / you / do?
   ....
5 We / not do / anything.
   ....
6 Simon / watch / TV?
   ....
7 I / stand / at the top / of the mountain.
   ....
8 Jamie and Kendra / leave / right now.
   ....

5 **Correct the mistake in each sentence.**
   walking
1 I'm ~~walk~~ to work at the moment.
2 Theo's swiming in the sea.
3 I really not enjoying this film.
4 She's eat a sandwich.
5 Where's you going now?
6 Yes, I'm driveing back now.
7 Are you have a good time?
8 I think she's runing on the beach.

Vocabulary
Weather

1 Complete the table with the words in the box.

~~autumn~~ foggy hot raining snowing spring
summer winter

nouns	verbs	adjectives
autumn		

2 Choose the best option to match the description of the weather, a or b.

1 It's foggy.
   a I can't see very far.   b The sky is blue.
2 It's raining.
   a I need my sunglasses.   b I need an umbrella.
3 It's cold and wet.
   a Let's stay inside and watch a film.
   b Let's have a picnic.
4 It's hot.
   a I'm wearing warm clothes.   b I'm wearing shorts.
5 It's windy.
   a The trees are moving.   b We're lying on the beach.
6 It's cloudy and cool.
   a The sky is blue.
   b It's nice because yesterday was too hot.
7 It's snowing.
   a I'm wearing shorts.   b Everything is white.
8 It's warm and sunny.
   a We're having a picnic.   b Turn on the heating, please.

3 Complete the sentences with the words in the box.

autumn cloudy cold foggy hot raining
summer sunny windy winter

1 It only snows in the _____ here.
2 Come outside, it's warm and _____ .
3 I can't see anything because it's so _____ .
4 It feels cold outside because it's so _____ .
5 My favourite season is _____ when the leaves fall from the trees.
6 Oh no! It's _____ outside and I don't have an umbrella.
7 It's _____ , so I'm wearing shorts.
8 It's a lovely day and the sky is blue. It feels like _____ , but it's only February!
9 At the moment it's hot in the day, but it's very _____ at night.
10 It was very sunny this morning, but now the sky is _____ .

Grammar
Present simple and present continuous

4 Match the sentence halves.

1 I usually have lunch outside, _____
2 I normally leave at 5 p.m., _____
3 Imogen usually gets the bus to work, _____
4 It's usually warm here in April, _____
5 I usually work in an office, _____
6 I don't often cook, _____
7 We don't usually like horror films, _____
8 Jack goes to school every day, _____

a but I'm trying to finish this report.
b but we're really enjoying this one.
c but today it's snowing!
d but it's raining today, so I'm eating inside.
e but today he's sick, so he's staying at home.
f but today I'm working from home.
g but it's my wife's birthday, so I'm making dinner.
h but today she's late, so she's driving.

5 Choose the correct alternatives.

1 What *do you do / are you doing* at the moment?
2 I always *drive / am driving* to work.
3 They *go / are going* to Spain for their holiday every year.
4 I *have / 'm having* dinner at the moment. Can I call you back?
5 Look outside – it *snows / 's snowing*!
6 What time *do you get up / are you getting up* in the week?
7 It's a lovely sunny day and the children *play / are playing* in the garden.
8 We *don't do / aren't doing* much on Sundays.

6 Complete the conversation with the verbs in brackets in the present simple or present continuous.

A: Where ¹_____ you _____ (work), Cathy?
B: I ²_____ (work) in the Birmingham office.
A: ³_____ you _____ (like) it there?
B: Yes, I do. At the moment we ⁴_____ (change) a lot of things though.
A: Like what?
B: Well, we ⁵_____ (introduce) a new computer system, so we ⁶_____ (learn) how to use that right now.
A: That sounds interesting.
B: It is, but it's also hard work. We ⁷_____ (work) long hours at the moment.
A: Ah, I understand. We always ⁸_____ (work) long hours in our office!

Vocabulary

Phrases describing travel

1 Cross out the alternative that is not correct.

1 get on the *bus/taxi/train*
2 arrive in *New York/the city/home*
3 leave *house/home/work*
4 stay at *a hotel/a guest house/a city*
5 book *a trip/somewhere by bus/a boat ride*
6 arrive at *bike/the airport/the shopping mall*
7 get off *a bike/home/the train*
8 go somewhere by *the airport/bus/metro*

2 Choose the correct option, a, b or c.

1 We arrived _____ the hotel at lunchtime.
   a at   b to   c –
2 You can take _____ a boat trip on the River Thames.
   a to   b for   c –
3 What time did you leave _____ home?
   a –   b from   c to
4 Andrew usually goes to work _____ bus.
   a for   b to   c by
5 When did they arrive _____ London?
   a in   b at   c –
6 We got _____ home late last night.
   a to   b back   c in
7 We need to get _____ this train.
   a to   b at   c on
8 We're staying _____ the Royal Hotel.
   a at   b on   c –
9 Do we need to book _____ a hotel for next week?
   a to   b on   c –
10 We need to get _____ the bus at the next stop.
   a off   b out   c of

3 Complete the message with the missing words.

● ● ●

Hi, Jan! I finally arrived ¹_____ Barcelona last night after a very long journey! It was terrible. I left home early, but there was a lot of traffic, so I arrived ²_____ the airport in London late and only just got ³_____ the plane with two minutes to go! But then we waited on the plane for a long time because there was a problem with the engine. After an hour, we got ⁴_____ the plane and onto a new one. We finally left London, but when we arrived ⁵_____ the city it was very late and there were no trains, so I took a taxi, which was very expensive. Anyway, I'm staying ⁶_____ the Garden Hotel. I think it's quite near you, so would you like to meet for a coffee?

Grammar

Superlative adjectives

4 Write the superlative forms of the adjectives.

1 old   *the oldest*
2 long   _____
3 nice   _____
4 expensive _____
5 busy   _____
6 good   _____
7 healthy   _____
8 beautiful _____
9 bad   _____
10 strange   _____

5 Complete the sentences with the superlative form of the adjectives in brackets.

1 _____ (easy) way to get around London is on the underground.
2 Summer is _____ (good) time of year, in my opinion.
3 What's _____ (cheap) way to travel in your country?
4 My dad is _____ (interesting) person I know.
5 Taxis are _____ (expensive) way to travel.
6 The morning is _____ (bad) time of day for me.
7 We live in _____ (noisy) part of the city.
8 Autumn is _____ (busy) time of year for us.
9 Café Forno does _____ (delicious) breakfast in town.
10 _____ (safe) way to travel is by plane.

6 Use the prompts to write superlative sentences.

1 My grandma / nice / person I know.
   My grandma is the nicest person I know.
2 The Nile / long / river in Africa.
   _____
3 Rahma's / expensive / restaurant in the city.
   _____
4 That hotel / bad / in New York.
   _____
5 Tokyo is / large / city in Japan.
   _____
6 This / busy / time of day for us.
   _____
7 My daughter / beautiful / girl in the world.
   _____
8 This is / big / shopping centre in Europe.
   _____

8D

Functional language
Make a phone call

1 Put the words in the correct order to make sentences or questions.

1 taxi, / please / I / a / book / Could / ?
   Could I book a taxi, please?

2 again / Sorry, / you / that / say / can / ?

3 much / help / Thanks / your / for / very / .

4 table / window / Do / mean / you / the / the / near / ?

5 Surgery / Hello, / Greenfields / .

6 appointment / I / Can / an / with / make / Dr Sanders / ?

7 that / didn't / I / hear / Sorry, / .

8 you / soon / See / .

2 Complete the conversations with the words in the box.

again	book	for	hear	make	mean
See	soon	speaking	Thanks	that	

1 **A:** Sorry, can you say that .... ?
   B: Yes, it's GREEN Street.

2 **A:** Hello, is .... the Chox Grill restaurant?
   B: Yes, it is. How can I help?

3 **A:** .... you on Friday at four o'clock.
   B: Thanks .... your help.

4 **A:** Do you .... the café on Farm Road?
   B: Yes, that's right.

5 **A:** .... very much for your help.
   B: You're welcome. See you ....

6 **A:** Sorry, I didn't .... that.
   B: It's 541773.

7 **A:** Could I .... a taxi, please?
   B: Yes, of course. Where are you going?

8 **A:** Hello, Acton Road Surgery. Clive ....
   B: Hi, can I .... an appointment with the dentist, please?

8

Listening

1 🔊 8.01 Listen to an interview with a man cycling around the world. Tick the questions the interviewer asks.

1 Where are you at the moment?
2 What are you doing right now?
3 Why did you decide to cycle around the world?
4 What's a typical day for you?
5 What do you eat?
6 How is this trip different from other types of travel?
7 How far do you cycle each day?
8 Where do you sleep?
9 Where are you going next?
10 What advice can you give for someone who wants to cycle around the world?

2 Listen again. Match Kevin's answers a–f with the questions in Exercise 1.

a I didn't like my job. ....
b Outside. ....
c I'm in Argentina. ....
d Try it first and see if you like it. ....
e 100 km or more. ....
f I get up early, have breakfast then cycle. ....

3a Are the sentences true (T) or false (F)?

1 The weather is warm and sunny where Kevin is. ....
2 Kevin thought his job was boring. ....
3 He wanted to travel. ....
4 He has a very big breakfast every day. ....
5 He cycles exactly 100 km every day. ....
6 He cycled over 200 km one day. ....
7 He usually travels in winter. ....
8 He likes watching TV in the evenings. ....
9 He suggests doing small trips before big ones. ....
10 He thinks this is the best way to travel. ....

b Listen again and check.

4 Match the words/phrases in bold in extracts 1–5 with meanings a–e.

1 ... so I'm having a **break** from the trip for a day or two. ....
2 I had a boring **desk job** ... .
3 What's a **typical** day for you? ....
4 I try to cycle **at least** 100 km a day. ....
5 I really enjoy a **camp fire** and having dinner outside at the end of a long day of cycling. ....

a usual
b a stop for a short time
c a fire outside which you can cook on
d a job in an office
e not less than

Reading

1 **Read the introduction to an article. What is it about?**
  a interesting and unusual types of weather
  b how we talk about the weather
  c weather we all hate

2 **Read the whole article and answer the questions.**
  What type(s) of weather ...
  1 can you only see at night?
  2 happens after a storm at sea?
  3 happens during a storm?
  4 is dangerous for planes?
  5 are in the shape of a circle?
  6 are common in parts of the US?

3 **Read the article again. Are the sentences true (T) or false (F)?**
  1 Lenticular clouds often form near mountains. ....
  2 Airplanes can fly through lenticular clouds easily. ....
  3 Moonbows appear in the daytime. ....
  4 It isn't possible to see moonbows in the US. ....
  5 Catatumbo lightning appears in Venezuela. ....
  6 Halos only appear in very hot places. ....
  7 Halos are always white. ....
  8 A Cappuccino coast appears when the sea is calm. ....

4 **Match the words in bold in the article with meanings a–e.**
  a when the moon is a full circle
    ....
  b strange objects in the sky that some people believe are from another world ....
  c a collection of a lot of very small bubbles on top of water ....
  d when the sun goes down at the end of the day ....
  e strong movements of air in the sky
    ....

Weather around the world

Everyone likes talking about the weather. We're always too hot, too cold or too wet. It seems we're never happy. However, the weather around the world can produce some beautiful and awesome things. Here we look at five of them.

Lenticular clouds

These clouds are round. People often think they're **UFOs**! They are different from any other type of cloud because you can see them anywhere and they don't move. They're most common in areas with lots of mountains. Pilots try not to fly near them because the **turbulence** they create is very strong, so it's dangerous to fly near them.

Moonbows

We all know about rainbows, the beautiful, colourful things in the sky created when the sun shines through water in the air. But did you know that there are moonbows, too? These appear on nights with a **full moon**, usually around two to three hours after **sunset**. The most common places to see them are Yosemite National Park in the US, Plitvice Lakes in Croatia, and Victoria Falls in Zambia/Zimbabwe.

Catatumbo lightning

Some people describe where the Catatumbo River meets Lake Maracaibo in Venezuela as the most electric place on earth. There is powerful lightning for about half of the year, for ten hours a day and sometimes up to 280 times an hour! During storms, lightning comes down from clouds almost a kilometre high in the sky. It usually forms above the area where the river meets the lake.

Halos

You can see a halo anywhere in the world. Very small pieces of ice very high in the sky make a circle around the sun or the moon. There are a lot of different types and they can be white or coloured.

Cappuccino coast

This happens when there are strong storms out at sea. They then produce a **foam** near the coast which makes the water look like a delicious cappuccino! Unfortunately, the water mixes up salts, chemicals and dead animals and plants, so they're not delicious like a cappuccino! They're common on the coast of San Francisco in the US, and the North Sea in Europe.

Writing

1 Read Tamara's email. What does she want?

From: Tamara Walker
To: Lucija Babić

Hi, Lucija! How are you? I'm coming to Croatia for my holiday in September and I thought of you. Can you recommend any places to visit?

Thanks, and let's meet when I'm there. ☺

---

2 Read Lucija's reply and answer the questions.

1 Why is September a good time to visit?

2 Where does she recommend?

3 What can you do there?

4 How long is the ticket for?

5 What should she bring?

6 What must visitors NOT do in the park?

From: Lucija Babić
To: Tamara Walker

Hi, Tamara. So good to hear from you! September is a very good time to come here because the weather is perfect. It's warm and really sunny, but it's not too hot.

Do you know where exactly you'll be? I can definitely recommend Plitvice Lakes. Attached is a photo of them.

It's the oldest and largest national park in Croatia and the area is beautiful. It is in the heart of Croatia, between two areas of mountains. You can go hiking around the lakes on one of the trails and enjoy the awesome views everywhere. You can also take a boat trip around the lakes, which is a really nice way to explore the area. The park is mostly forest and you can see lots of really interesting plants and animals around. In the winter there is excellent skiing in the area, too, but you won't be here then. Next time, maybe!

You can drive to the main park and buy a ticket to enter. This ticket is for the whole day. You need to wear the right clothes and shoes for hiking though, and don't walk off the trails or swim in the lakes. This is to protect the wildlife. Oh, and bring some sun cream and a good hat!

I really hope you visit Plitvice Lakes, it's a wonderful place and a beautiful part of the country. Definitely contact me when you're here, I'd really like to see you again!

---

3 Read the Focus box. How can you make your writing more interesting?

Using adjectives

Use adjectives to make your writing more interesting.

- Use 'strong' adjectives, e.g. *delicious, wonderful, awesome, amazing, fantastic, beautiful.*
  *... because the weather is **perfect**.*
- Use words like *very* and *really* to make weak adjectives (like *good, bad, nice, interesting, exciting*) stronger.
  *September is a **very good** time to come here, ...*

4 Cross out the alternative which is not correct.

1 It's a very *nice/ delicious/ interesting* dish.
2 Spring is a very *good/ nice/ awesome* time to visit.
3 Enjoy the *fantastic/ beautiful/ delicious* view at the top of the mountain.
4 There are a lot of really *very/ interesting/ pretty* animals to see.
5 It's a very *exciting/ wonderful/ nice* part of the country.
6 That was a very *bad/ terrible/ boring* film.

Prepare

5 You're going to write a recommendation for a place to visit that you know well. Choose a place and make notes on these things:
- where it is
- why you like it
- what you can do there
- advice for visiting there

Write

6 Write your recommendation. Use your notes in Exercise 5 and the Focus box to help you.

9A

Vocabulary

Health

1 Choose the correct alternatives.

1 How can I *stay/eat* healthy?
2 Don't buy a burger again for lunch. You need to *do/eat* well.
3 How much does it cost to *join/keep* a gym?
4 Ssh! *Go/Keep* to sleep, it's late!
5 We *walked/moved* around the shops for an hour or two.
6 What do you do to *do/keep* fit?
7 *Stand/Sit* down and make yourself comfortable.
8 I need to *have/do* some exercise. I might go running.

2 Match the sentence halves.

1 I want you to stand _____
2 It's only one floor; let's walk _____
3 We always eat _____
4 Do you go _____
5 Playing sport is a good way to do _____
6 At work, try to move _____
7 Try not to sit _____
8 Running is an excellent way to keep _____

a up the stairs.
b down all day.
c fit.
d up and find a partner.
e around every hour or so.
f well – lots of salad and vegetables.
g to sleep as soon as you go to bed?
h some exercise.

3 Complete the conversations with the missing words.

1 **A:** How do you keep _____?
   B: I try to _____ some exercise every day, like sport or running.
   A: I don't like either of those.
   B: Well, why don't you join a _____?

2 **A:** I sit _____ at my desk all day. I don't think it's good for me.
   B: Yes, you're right. Why don't you stand _____ and walk around more often?
   A: I forget to do that.
   B: You can use this app, look. It reminds you to do it every hour. I use it and I move _____ much more every day.
   A: Nice! That's how you manage to stay _____ then?
   B: Yes, and I eat _____ .

Grammar

should/shouldn't

4 Match problems 1–8 with advice a–h.

1 I'm bored.
2 I haven't got any money.
3 I need to get there quickly.
4 It's raining.
5 I'm always tired.
6 I've got a big exam next week.
7 I haven't got any friends.
8 I want to learn to play the guitar.

a You should take an umbrella.
b You should watch a film.
c You should join a club.
d You should go to bed early.
e You should have lessons.
f You should get a job.
g You should study.
h You should take a taxi.

5 Complete the sentences with *should* or *shouldn't*.

1 You _____ eat lots of sugar. It's bad for you.
2 What time _____ we leave? I don't want to arrive late.
3 You _____ study for your exam next week. It's important.
4 You _____ watch TV in bed. It doesn't help you sleep.
5 She's always tired. She _____ go to bed so late.
6 You _____ take a coat. It's cold outside.
7 You _____ stay out so late when you have school the next day.
8 _____ we take a bus or a train?

6 Correct the mistake in each sentence.

1 We should ~~to~~ take a present to the party.

2 Should I calling Simone?

3 You shouldn't talking to Richard like that.

4 Do we should leave early?

5 You shouldn't to eat so fast.

6 She should doing more exercise.

7 Should I to ask Ines?

8 I shouldn't ate so much.

Grammar

be going to

1 **Put the words in the correct order to make sentences or questions.**

1 buy / She's / to / a / phone / going / mobile / .
   She's going to buy a mobile phone.

2 be / to / They're / going / late / .
   ....

3 get / to / there / aren't / We / going / on time /.
   ....

4 at / Are / you / stay / home / going / to / today / ?
   ....

5 to / isn't / late / She / work / going / .
   ....

6 I'm / to / going / language / learn / another / .
   ....

7 to / you / are / leave / time / going / What / ?
   ....

8 chocolate / I'm / eat / not / to / this month / going / .
   ....

2 **Correct the mistake in each sentence.**

             to
1 It isn't going ⁄ be easy.

2 Going are you to see Sam?

3 What time are you go to get up tomorrow?

4 James and Chiara is going to have lunch together.

5 We aren't going to being late, don't worry.

6 What are you going do at the weekend?

7 I'm not going doing anything!

8 We going to watch a film at the cinema.

3 **Use the prompts to write sentences with *going to*.**

1 It / rain / weekend.
   It's going to rain at the weekend.

2 You / be / late.
   ....

3 I / try / a new recipe.
   ....

4 We / not have / holiday this year.
   ....

5 They / visit / Bangkok next summer.
   ....

6 She / not get married.
   ....

Vocabulary

Future plans

4 **Match verbs 1–8 with phrases a–h.**

1	do	a	where to go
2	look	b	a course
3	decide	c	how to do something
4	buy	d	a new book
5	save	e	to people at work
6	learn	f	for a job
7	get	g	a new job
8	talk	h	money

5 **Choose the correct alternatives.**

1 I'd like to *study/ learn* how to play the guitar.

2 Jamie is *doing/ learning* a course in French.

3 Did you *look/ talk* to Sally last night?

4 Can you help me *look/ save* for my keys? I can't find them.

5 How can I *buy/ save* money each month?

6 I need to *do/ buy* a new shirt for work.

7 I'm trying to *look/ get* a new job.

8 We need to *decide/ talk* what to do for Sean's birthday.

6 **Complete the sentences with the missing words.**

1 We're going to .... a bonus at the end of the year.

2 I'd like to .... a new language this year.

3 Can you help me .... where to go for my next holiday?

4 Plan your writing – it can .... time later.

5 I'm going to .... to Julian at the conference.

6 I need to .... more exercise, so I'm going to join a gym.

7 You need to .... for a job.

8 I got some money for my birthday, so I'm going to .... a new computer.

Vocabulary

Activities with *go*

1 **Choose the correct alternatives.**

1 We're going *skiing/surfing* in the mountains near my house.

2 Sometimes we go *swimming/horse riding* in the lake.

3 Tina's going *climbing/shopping* at the new sports centre.

4 Last year we went *surfing/sightseeing* in Prague. I took some amazing photos!

5 Last winter they went *swimming/skiing* in the mountains.

6 There's lots to do at the shopping centre. You can go *bowling/cycling* or watch a film at the cinema.

7 Every Sunday I go *cycling/shopping* in the countryside with a group of friends.

8 I'd like to go *shopping/climbing* in the mountains.

2 **Complete the sentences with the activities in the box.**

> climbing   cycling   horse riding   shopping
> sightseeing   snowboarding   surfing   swimming

1 I'd like to go ...., but I'm scared I might fall off if it runs fast!

2 When I'm on holiday, I like to go .... around different cities, visiting famous places.

3 When we went to Hawaii, we went .... every day. We were in the sea all day.

4 Let's go .... at the new pool in town.

5 Last weekend I went .... at a huge department store with my friend.

6 In Amsterdam you can go .... around the city on the cycle paths.

7 A lot of people like to go .... on this mountain in the summer.

8 Every winter we go .... in the Alps. It's cold, but it's great fun.

Grammar

would like/want

3 **Choose the correct alternatives.**

1 **A:** Where do you *want/like* to go this afternoon?
   B: I'd *like/want* to go to the shops.

2 **A:** Let's go to the cinema.
   B: No, I *not/don't* want to. There's nothing interesting on.
   A: OK, well what *you want/do you want* to do?

3 **A:** *Do/Would* you like to come to my party on Saturday?
   B: I *want to/want* come, but I'm not here then.

4 **A:** Farah *wants/want* to learn a new language.
   B: Really? What language *do/does* she want to learn?
   A: I think she'd *like/want* to learn German.

5 **A:** Who *would you/you would* like to sit with?
   B: I *want/would* to sit next to Maisy. We always sit together.

4 **Make the sentences negative.**

1 I want to go swimming.
   I don't want to go swimming.

2 Janice would like to watch a horror film.

3 He wants to travel by bus.

4 I'd like to go to Iceland.

5 They want to go to a museum.

6 I want to learn how to play the piano.

7 Paulo wants to find a new job.

8 You'd like to go to a salsa class.

5 **Correct the mistake in each sentence.**

1 I'd like ~~go~~ *to* go to the cinema.

2 Sheila want to go on holiday.

3 Want you to come to my party?

4 My parents wouldn't like to eating sushi.

5 I wouldn't liking to get up that early.

6 I want learning how to cook.

7 My wife would likes to visit Paris.

8 I not want to try anything new.

Functional language

Make arrangements and invitations

1 Match the sentence halves.

1 What shall _____
2 Good _____
3 Do you want _____
4 Where shall _____
5 Sorry I can't, _____
6 I don't think _____
7 Let's _____
8 Would you _____
9 What time _____
10 I'm not _____

a to join us?
b it's a good idea.
c we do to celebrate?
d sure.
e idea!
f shall we meet?
g we meet?
h I'm busy.
i cook a meal.
j like to come?

2 Complete the conversations with the missing words.

1 **A:** What _____ we do to celebrate passing our exams?
   B: _____ go bowling!
   A: Good _____! Hey Jan, we're going to go bowling at the weekend. Would you _____ to come?
   C: Yes, _____!

2 **A:** _____ shall we meet?
   B: At the café?
   A: I don't _____ it's a good idea. It's too far away.
   B: What about the station then?
   A: Yes, that's better.
   B: What _____ shall we meet?
   A: Seven o'clock?
   B: OK.

3 **A:** Hi, James. We're going to have a picnic on Sunday. Do you want to _____ us?
   B: Sorry, I can't, I'm _____.
   A: That's a shame. We're going to have a party on Saturday, too. Would you like to _____?
   B: _____, please! I'd love to.

Listening

1 ◁)) 9.01 **Listen to a conversation between two friends. What two pieces of advice does Magda give Chris?**

2 Listen again. Are the sentences true (T) or false (F)?
1 Chris wants to try a new diet. _____
2 You can't eat cheese on the diet. _____
3 Magda thinks the diet sounds good. _____
4 Chris doesn't want to stop eating bread. _____
5 Magda says Chris should do something that helps him get slim quickly. _____
6 Chris wants to go cycling. _____
7 Magda says Chris should only eat healthy food. _____
8 She suggests using an app. _____

3a Choose the correct option, a or b.
1 Chris talks about a diet with _____ fat.
   a a lot of   b very little
2 The diet includes _____ bread.
   a a lot of   b a little
3 Magda thinks 'fad' diets are _____.
   a healthy   b unhealthy
4 Magda thinks Chris should _____ more often.
   a exercise   b eat
5 She says he should have _____ meals.
   a smaller   b bigger
6 She suggests using an app to _____ what he eats.
   a record   b improve

b Listen again and check.

4 Match the words/phrases in extracts 1–3 with meanings a–c.
1 It sounds like a **fad** to me. _____
2 Think about the **long term**. _____
3 That way it can be part of your everyday **routine**. _____

a the usual order which you do things
b happening for a long time
c something that is popular for a short time

Reading

1 Read the introduction to the article. What are 'ultra-marathons'?

a marathons shorter than 42 km

b marathons equal to 42 km

c marathons longer than 42 km

2 Read the rest of the article and put the topics in the correct order.

a her future plans _____

b how she started running _____

c advice for new runners _____

d what she likes most and least _____

3 Read the article again. Choose the correct option, a or b.

1 Lucy Wilkins runs _____ .
  a in the UK
  b in different countries

2 When she first started, she _____ .
  a walked   b ran and walked

3 Her first race was _____ .
  a 5 km   b a marathon

4 After that she _____ increased the distance she ran.
  a slowly   b quickly

5 Her race in France was _____ than a marathon.
  a shorter   b longer

6 She likes running because it's _____ to do.
  a easy   b challenging

7 She doesn't like thinking about _____ .
  a food   b clothes

8 The race in California is going to be _____ than her other races.
  a shorter   b longer

9 She _____ she's going to finish it.
  a thinks   b doesn't think

10 She says you need to start running _____ .
  a slowly   b quickly

4 Match the words/phrases in bold in the article with meanings 1–4.

1 easy _____

2 difficult, but interesting _____

3 do something slowly _____

4 a competition to see who or what is the fastest _____

In the long run

Lucy Wilkins runs ultra-marathons (marathons longer than 42 km). She lives in Hull in the northeast of England, but travels all over the world to run in **challenging** places. Here she talks to us about her running.

'I first started running in 2014. At first I was very slow and I walked a little, then I ran a little. Slowly I started to run for a longer time. Then I entered my first **race** – it was a 5 km race near home and I loved it. I wasn't very fast, but I really enjoyed running with lots of other people. Then I slowly increased the distance I ran and I entered my first marathon (42 km) two years later. I felt so good after that. Then I started to run longer distances. In 2017 I entered a 60 km race in the mountains in France, which lasted for 30 hours. It was very difficult, but I felt so good at the end.

I love being alone with my thoughts when I run. I also love the feeling I have at the end. I feel like I've really done something good for myself and for my body. It's such a **simple** thing, too, just putting one foot in front of the other. I don't like having to be careful about what I eat before a run though. You have to get it just right: not too much and not too little. If you get it wrong, you can feel really sick.

At the moment I'm training for a race in the US, in California. It's going to be my longest yet – 100 km! I'm sure I'm going to finish it, but I know it's going to be hard.

My main advice for anyone who wants to do long-distance running is to enjoy it! Slowly increase how far you run. **Take your time** and enjoy the countryside!'

Writing

1 Read Paulo's email. What is he going to do in the summer?

From: Paulo Costas
To: Simon Wilson

Hi Simon,

How are things with you? Hope you had a good new year.

I have some exciting news to tell you about. This summer I'm going to visit London and stay for two months. I'm going to study English at a school in Fulham. Is that near you? I'm really excited about it because it's going to be my first time in London. I'm going to study in the mornings and then in the afternoons I'd like to go sightseeing and visit different places.

What about you? Are you going to be in London? Maybe we can meet and have a coffee or something. Let me know when you're free.

Bye for now.

Paulo

---

2 Read the email again and answer the questions.

1 How long is Paulo going to stay in London?

2 Where in London is he going to study?

3 What's he going to do in the mornings?

4 What's he going to do in the afternoons?

5 What does he want Simon to do with him there?

3 Read the Focus box and underline points 1–5 in the email in Exercise 1.

Organising an email to a friend

1 Begin with a greeting, e.g.
Hi Simon, Hello Charlotte!
2 Ask an opening question or comment, e.g.
How are you?
Hope you had a good weekend/New Year/holiday.
Good to hear from you! (if your email is a reply)
3 Introduce your news, e.g.
I have some exciting news to tell you about.
4 Ask follow-up questions or requests, e.g.
What about you? Let me know (when you're free).
5 End with a closing phrase, e.g.
All the best, Bye for now,
Love to the children/Fiona/your mum.

4 Match phrases a–e with points 1–5 in the Focus box.
a See you soon. ....
b Anyway, I have some news. ....
c How are things with you? ....
d Hello Kim, ...
e Please write and tell me your news. ....

Prepare

5 You're going to write an email to a friend telling them about a plan you have for next year. Choose one of these things:
• a holiday or trip
• a course
• a new hobby/sport
• your own idea

6 Plan your email using the following structure:
• Say hello.
• Ask a question or make a comment.
• Describe your plan.
• Ask a follow-up question.
• Close the email.

Write

7 Write your email. Use your plan from Exercise 6 and the Focus box to help you.

Vocabulary

Housework

1 Match 1–7 with a–g.

1	do the	a	your room
2	fix	b	washing-up
3	share	c	for people
4	do	d	things
5	clean	e	the bathroom
6	tidy	f	the bills
7	cook	g	the laundry

2 Choose the correct alternatives.

1 Can somebody *wash up/clean up* some plates, please?
2 I've got no clean clothes! I need to *tidy/do* the laundry.
3 You can play video games after you *tidy/wash* your room.
4 Let's *do/cook* mum a meal for her birthday.
5 Can you help me *fix/share* some things in my house?
6 In this house we *share/do* all the bills.
7 Can you *wash/clean* the bathroom, please? It's very dirty.

3 Complete the 'House Rules'.

House Rules

① Everyone shares the _____. It doesn't matter how much energy you use.

② Everyone usually cooks _____ the other people in the house once a month. This isn't a rule, but it's nice! ☺

③ Tidy your own _____.

④ We take turns to clean the _____. Check the chart above the bath.

⑤ Do your own _____. Instructions for the washing machine are on the side.

⑥ Do your washing _____ immediately after you cook. Don't leave it for someone else!

⑦ Is something broken? Call Mike on 2384 2317065. He fixes _____ for us.

Grammar

Verb patterns

4 Complete the conversations with the correct form of the verbs in the boxes.

1 | clean do tidy wash |

A: Do you mind _____ the bathroom?
B: Oh, I hate _____ that. I don't mind _____ your room for you though.
A: OK, that's nice. There are some dirty dishes in there though. Do you mind _____ them up?
B: No problem.

2 | do (x2) go sit watch |

A: What do you like _____ in your free time?
B: I like _____ out with my friends. What about you?
A: Oh, not much. I like _____ on the sofa and _____ TV.
B: That's me on Sundays. I love _____ nothing at all!

3 | be do have meet talk work |

A: What do you like about your job?
B: I like _____ to the customers every day and I like the people I work with. I don't like _____ at the weekend though.
A: I don't mind _____ at work at the weekend. What do you like _____ at the weekend?
B: I love _____ up with friends and _____ a pizza or something.

5 Use the prompts to write sentences or questions.

1 you / like / visit museums?
   Do you like visiting museums?
2 What / you / like / do / weekend?
   _____
3 I / not like / travel / bus.
   _____
4 Farah / not mind / clean / bathroom.
   _____
5 We / love / sit / in / park.
   _____
6 you / mind / open / window?
   _____
7 My dad / hate / cook.
   _____
8 What subject / you / like / study / school?
   _____
9 they / mind / share / bills?
   _____
10 My parents / not like / stay / home.
   _____

10B

Vocabulary

Clothes

1 Find 12 words for clothes in the wordsearch.

S	T	C	A	I	N	T	T	R	A	N	S
T	R	A	I	N	E	R	S	R	J	S	O
A	R	P	I	N	E	O	F	Y	T	I	E
S	I	O	E	N	E	U	E	A	S	T	E
B	O	O	T	S	F	S	J	E	R	C	S
I	O	P	R	D	R	E	S	S	E	B	U
V	C	R	E	E	O	R	S	S	T	Y	I
O	J	I	R	T	M	S	S	H	I	R	T
H	E	L	M	E	T	N	C	O	R	E	T
Y	A	E	U	N	I	F	O	R	M	A	X
E	N	R	I	E	F	R	A	T	F	O	R
S	S	N	U	N	I	T	T	S	O	R	F

2 Which of the clothes in Exercise 1 do you wear ...

1 on your head?
2 on your legs?
3 on your feet?
4 on your whole body?

3 Choose the correct alternatives.

1 Do you have to wear *smart clothes/a helmet* in the office?
2 Put your *shorts/coat* on. It's cold outside.
3 Have you got a *dress/tie* I can borrow to wear with my shirt?
4 I've got a job interview! Now I need to buy *a suit/jeans*.
5 It's lovely weather, so I'm going to put my *suit/shorts* on.
6 These *trousers/shorts* are too short. You can see my legs!
7 Put your *helmet/tie* on before you ride your bike.
8 The best thing about summer is wearing a *dress/coat*.
9 I usually just wear *jeans/a uniform* at home.
10 I work in a big supermarket, so I have to wear a *uniform/suit*.

Grammar

have to/don't have to

4 Choose the correct alternatives.

1 A: Do we *have/has* to share the bills?
   B: Yes, but we don't *have/has* to pay for electricity.
2 A: *Do/Does* Maria have to wear a uniform?
   B: No, but she *have/has* to work on Sundays.
3 A: What time do we have *to get/getting* to work tomorrow?
   B: Well, I *have/has* to be here at 8 a.m., but you *don't/not* have to be here until 9.30.
4 A: You have to *tidying/tidy* your room, now.
   B: Oh Mum, *do I have/have I* to?
5 A: What time *you have/do you have* to be there?
   B: Nine o'clock. Oh dear, I *have to/have* leave now!

5 Complete the sentences with the correct form of (*don't*) *have to* and the verbs in brackets.

1 What do you _____*have to do*_____ (do) today?
2 Carla _____ (drive) to work today.
3 We _____ (not answer) emails immediately.
4 Do we _____ (wear) a suit?
5 I _____ (get up) at 4 a.m. tomorrow!
6 He _____ (not practise) every day.
7 You _____ (study) for your exam tomorrow.
8 I _____ (not be) there until four o'clock.
9 You _____ have a passport when you travel to another country.
10 She _____ (not have) a certificate.

6 Use the notes to complete the sentences with (*don't*) *have to*.

1 Work Monday – Friday.
   You _____*don't have to*_____ work at the weekend.
2 Arrive at 5 a.m.
   We _____ get there early.
3 Wear jeans and a T-shirt.
   I _____ wear smart clothes.
4 Take your driving licence.
   You _____ take your passport.
5 No public transport.
   She _____ have a car.
6 Leave in five minutes.
   They _____ leave soon.
7 Finish work at 1 p.m.
   Harry _____ work late.
8 The bathroom's dirty.
   You _____ clean the bathroom.
9 The report isn't finished.
   I _____ write a report.
10 He's got a car.
   He _____ travel by bus.

Vocabulary

Technology

1 Cross out the alternative that is not correct.

1 *open / close / own / ~~save~~* a laptop
2 own a *tablet / file / printer / smartphone*
3 download a(n) *website / app / program / file*
4 *read / write / go / send* a message
5 *visit / look for / go / read* a website
6 go *online / on the internet / online game*
7 play a(n) *online game / website / multiplayer game*
8 save a *file / screen / program / message*

2 Choose the correct option, a or b.

1 Do you like my new _____? They're really loud!
   a speakers   b tablets
2 I like _____ games that you play online with thousands of people.
   a website   b multiplayer
3 I always carry my _____ with me – even in the bathroom!
   a smartphone   b printer
4 Where can I _____ that file from?
   a download   b close
5 I'm _____ for a website with information on flights.
   a reading   b looking
6 _____ me a message when you get home, OK?
   a Send   b Open
7 Do you know how to write a _____?
   a file   b program
8 The link should be at the top of the _____.
   a laptop   b screen
9 This _____ shows you where there are cafés near you.
   a app   b text message
10 My _____'s broken. It doesn't print in colour.
   a smartphone   b printer

3 Complete the sentences with the words in the box.

download	message	own	play	read	save
tablet	website				

1 I check their _____ every morning.
2 Don't forget to _____ your work so you don't lose it.
3 I use my _____ for watching films, but I use my laptop for work because it's got a keyboard.
4 I _____ online games every night.
5 I _____ your message, thanks.
6 Do you _____ a laptop?
7 You can _____ the app for free from our website.
8 Send me a _____ when you're outside.

Grammar

Present perfect simple

4 Put the words in the correct order to make sentences or questions.

1 to / I've / been / Alaska / never / .
   I've never been to Alaska.
2 a / ever / you / Have / video / made / ?
3 the report / Kieran / finished / has / .
4 Italian / I've / eaten / never / food / .
5 to / Has / she / been / Brazil / ever / ?
6 eaten / I've / meat / never / .
7 before / this / you / Have / film / seen / ?
8 the / You / done / haven't / washing-up / !
9 done / you / What / have / ?
10 a / never / I've / competition / won / .

5 Correct the mistake in each sentence.

             Have you
1 ~~You have~~ ever driven for longer than eight hours?
2 She has have a meeting with her manager.
3 I've never fly in a helicopter.
4 Have they went there before?
5 He's never tried Indian food.
6 I haven't finish my breakfast yet.
7 Myra hasn't never run a marathon.
8 We never gone fishing.

6 Use the prompts to write sentences and questions.

1 I / see / that film twice.
   I've seen that film twice.
2 you / ever / ride / a motorbike?
3 I / never / work / in a restaurant.
4 We / chat / online / few times.
5 you / ever / write / computer program?

Functional language
Give a compliment

1 Choose the correct alternatives.

1 **A:** I *like/ likes* your dress.
 B: *Thanks/ Thank* you.
2 **A:** You sing really *well/ good*.
 B: That's nice *of/ for* you to say.
3 **A:** You always *have/ make* me laugh.
 B: Thanks!
4 **A:** Your new car *looks like/ looks* great.
 B: I'm glad you *like/ like* it.
5 **A:** *This/ These* room is lovely!
 B: That's kind *for/ of* you.
6 **A:** You're *so/ such* helpful!
 B: Thanks!

2 Match the sentence halves.

1 You always tell ....
2 I'm pleased ....
3 You did ....
4 This food ....
5 You're ....
6 That's nice ....
7 The house looks ....
8 You play ....

a the best stories.
b is delicious!
c a fantastic job.
d really well.
e of you.
f great.
g you like it.
h so interesting.

3 Complete the conversations with the missing words.

1 **A:** You're .... kind.
 B: Thank ....
2 **A:** I love .... bag.
 B: I'm glad you like ....
3 **A:** You did a great ....
 B: That's nice of you to ....
4 **A:** Your new sofa .... lovely.
 B: I'm pleased .... like it.
5 **A:** You .... make me laugh.
 B: Thanks.
6 **A:** You dance really ....
 B: .... kind of you.

Listening

1 🔊 10.01 **Listen to a radio programme about technology and communication. Choose the correct option.**

a The speakers agree.   b The speakers disagree.

2 Listen again. Are the sentences true (T) or false (F)?

1 Scott thinks we communicate more with technology. ....
2 He says his son never talks to him. ....
3 Amelia thinks Scott's son doesn't talk to anyone in the evening. ....
4 Scott thinks it's OK to play video games all the time. ....
5 Scott likes playing online games. ....
6 Amelia thinks we communicate with more people because of technology. ....
7 Scott thinks text messages are a good way to communicate. ....
8 Amelia thinks technology helps us meet new people. ....

3a Choose the correct option, a or b.

1 Scott's son plays video games every ....
 a day   b weekend
2 Amelia thinks we communicate .... than before.
 a less   b more
3 Scott thinks communication these days is .... the past.
 a the same as   b different from
4 Scott .... played an online game.
 a has   b hasn't
5 Amelia knows someone who got married to someone they met ....
 a on social media   b at work
6 Scott thinks phone calls are .... than text messages.
 a better   b worse

b Listen again and check.

4 Match the words/phrases in bold in extracts 1–3 with meanings a–c.

1 My teenage son is **really into** video games. ....
2 So you actually **communicate with** people ... .
3 I think **the quality** of communication these days is worse. ....

a how good or bad something is
b interested in
c share information with someone

Reading

1 Read the article quickly and choose the best title.

  a Four ways to have a good house share
  b Four types of people who share a house
  c Four things NOT to do when sharing a house

2 Read the article again and match paragraphs 1–4 with headings a–e. There is one extra heading you do not need.

  a Communication is important
  b Keep it tidy
  c Don't eat other people's food
  d Sharing bills
  e Be nice

3 Read the article again. Are the sentences true (T) or false (F)?

  1 You should tidy your room every day. ....
  2 Everyone in the house should do the cleaning. ....
  3 It's easier to wash up dishes just after you use them. ....
  4 Decide how to share bills after a few months. ....
  5 You don't need to keep a record of things people buy for the house. ....
  6 You can leave messages for each other in the kitchen. ....
  7 You should plan when visitors come. ....
  8 You should never do someone else's housework for them. ....

4 Match the words in bold in the article with meanings 1–4.

  1 a thing that you can write on with a special pen
  ....
  2 parts of a house that you all share
  ....
  3 arrive ....
  4 things you use to change the taste of food ....

1 ....

You can tidy your room when you want to, but think about the **communal areas** like the kitchen and living room. You need to share the cleaning with your flatmates, but also clean up after you use something yourself. It's a good idea to wash up immediately after eating. That way dishes and other things are easier to clean, too.

2 ....

Make sure you agree with your flatmates how to share the bills from the beginning. It's not just bills, there are other things it's a good idea to share, such as cleaning products and common **condiments** like salt, pepper, cooking oil, etc. Keep a chart for who pays what and when.

3 ....

It's a good idea to have a **whiteboard** somewhere like the kitchen where everybody can see it. You can write messages on it for each other when you're not there, and clean them off when everyone's read them. It's also a good idea to have a visitor calendar for when your friends or family come to stay. You don't want to be in the situation where two or more of you invite people to stay and when they **turn up** you realise you don't have any space.

4 ....

There are lots of ways to do this, from a simple 'please' and 'thank you' at the right times, to offering to help when others have a problem. If you have time, offer to do someone else's housework when they're busy. You might find you need their help one day!

Writing

1 Andrea has written an email to her old English teacher. Why is she writing to her teacher?

● ● ●

Dear Tina,

How are you? I'm thinking about going to London this summer to study English and I'd like to find a good course for me. I really liked studying with you before and I think you're a very good teacher. Could you recommend a course for me?

Here are some things that I'm looking for. I love playing pronunciation games – I'm a big fan of games and I think these are my favourite! I also really like the vocabulary activities which help me remember all the words and phrases we learn on a course.

I'm OK with studying grammar, but it's not my favourite thing. I understand it's important though, so I don't mind studying it in class.

I can't stand speaking in front of the class. I get nervous and sometimes don't know what to say, but I'm fine with speaking in small groups. I'm into music and I like listening to songs in class. That's really good fun.

I hope you can help me and perhaps we can meet for a coffee when I'm there?

Thanks

Andrea

2 Read the email again and answer the questions.
1 What does she love doing?
   _____
2 What does she like doing?
   _____
3 What doesn't she like doing?
   _____
4 What doesn't she mind doing?
   _____

3 Read the Focus box and underline similar phrases in Andrea's email.

Expressing likes and dislikes

a expressing likes, e.g.
I'm a big fan of, is/are my favourite, is really good fun, I'm into …
b saying you don't mind something, e.g.
I'm OK with … , I'm fine about …
c expressing dislikes, e.g.
I can't stand … , I'm not really into …

4 Match sentences 1–6 with categories a–c in the Focus box.
1 Homework is not a problem. ....
2 I don't mind you correcting me. ....
3 I really hate writing in class. ....
4 I'm really into pronunciation activities. ....
5 I'm not into walking around the class. ....
6 I really like games. ....

Prepare

5 You're going to write an email to someone to ask for recommendations for a course. Make notes about:
• things you like doing in class
• things you don't mind doing in class
• things you don't like doing in class
• any other important information

Write

6 Write your email. Use your notes in Exercise 5 and the Focus box to help you.

AUDIO SCRIPTS

UNIT 1   Recording 1

1

M = Manager   L = Louisa   C = Carla   R = Rob

M: Good morning, Louisa. This is Carla, our new staff member. Today is her first day.

L: Hi, Carla. I'm Louisa.

C: Hi, Louisa. Nice to meet you.

M: Can you introduce her to the team, please?

L: Yes, of course. So where are you from, Carla?

C: I'm from Italy. What about you?

L: I'm Spanish. Erm, Rob?

R: Yes?

L: This is Carla. She's a new staff member from Italy.

R: Hi, Carla. Nice to meet you. I'm Rob, I'm from Spain. And this is Janice and Alex.

C: Nice to meet you both.

2

T = Tom   S = Skyler   J = Joanne

T: Hi, I'm Tom.

S: Hi, Tom. Nice to meet you. I'm Skyler and this is Joanne.

T: Nice to meet you both. Where are you from?

S: I'm from the Sydney office. I'm Australian, but Joanne isn't. She's American, from the New York office. Where are you from, Tom?

T: Oh, that's interesting. I'm British, I work in the London office. What department are you in?

J: We're both in sales. What about you?

T: I'm in marketing.

3

M = Miguel   J = Jenny   C = Claudia

M: Hi, everyone. I'm Miguel.

J: Hi, Miguel. Nice to meet you. Is this your first salsa class?

M: Yes, it is. I love dancing.

J: Me too! Where are you from, Miguel?

M: Well, I live here in the UK, but I'm not from here. I'm from Mexico.

J: Oh, right. Well, I'm Jenny, this is Paul and this is Claudia – I think she's Mexican, too.

M: Oh really? Where are you from, Claudia?

C: Oaxaca.

M: Ah, OK. I'm from Mexico City. And you? Jenny? Paul? Where are you from?

J: We're from the UK. We live here in Manchester.

M: Great.

UNIT 2   Recording 1

P = Presenter   R = Russell   J = Jeanette

P: Welcome to Episode 93 of the *Family Talk* podcast. This week's topic is 'big families' – something both of my guests know all about. So, Russell, how many people are there in your family?

R: Eleven.

P: Wow, really? And who are they?

R: Well, of course, there's mum and dad. Mum is a manager in a big company, and dad's a mechanic.

P: OK.

R: And then I've got seven siblings – four brothers and three sisters.

P: Wait, er … mum, dad, eight children … that's only ten people?

R: Yes, but there's also Henry.

P: Um, who's Henry?

R: My cat! I think he's my favourite family member!

P: And what about you, Jeanette?

J: Oh, I don't have a cat or a dog.

P: Ha! Well, how many brothers and sisters have you got?

J: Oh, I haven't got any brothers or sisters.

P: Uh, OK. But have you got a big family?

J: Yes, I have. My mum's got three brothers, and my dad's got two sisters and two brothers.

P: OK.

J: And they've all got kids, you see. I've got, um, ten cousins I think.

P: Wow!

J: Yes, and we all live in the same town and see each other all the time. So, we're a big family really. It's a lot of fun.

P: Right. And who's your favourite family member?

J: Me, of course!

UNIT 3   Recording 1

P = Presenter   K = Karl

P: Today I'm with Karl Rogan, the American skier who's got three silver medals and two gold medals. Nice to meet you, Karl.

K: Thanks Anne, nice to meet you, too.

P: So, what's a normal day for you, Karl? What time do you usually get up?

K: Well, I get up at seven o'clock every morning.

P: Right.

K: I have breakfast – I usually have an omelette and some coffee – then I do a few chores at home. You know, wash my clothes, reply to emails, that kind of thing. At around half past eight, I go to the gym. I stay at the gym for about three hours.

P: Wow, OK! And what do you have for lunch?

K: Well, I always have a good lunch. Usually chicken, rice and salad or vegetables. Sometimes fish. It depends what I feel like.

P: OK.

K: Then in the afternoon I go skiing. I usually ski Monday to Friday because there aren't many people. I ski for around four hours in the afternoon, then I go home and have dinner and relax with my wife. We usually watch TV in the evening, and go to bed at ten o'clock.

P: Sounds like a busy life!

K: Well, yes it is a bit. But I always rest on Sunday. I think it's important for your body to recover. But even then I can't wait to go skiing again on Monday!

UNIT 4   Recording 1

1

We love this town. There are lots of parks and the children love playing there. There aren't a lot of cars, either, like in a big city, so the air is clean and it's safe to walk around.

2

There isn't anything for young people to do here. There aren't any clubs or nice cafés to meet friends. It's really boring and I can't wait to move away.

3

I like it here, it's nice and quiet, but there isn't much public transport, which is a problem for me. There aren't any trains and there's only one bus an hour. You really need to have a car here and I haven't got one, so that's a problem.

4

Some people think it's boring here, but I disagree. I think the people are very friendly. I've got great neighbours and we often meet and do things together. It's easy to make friends here, but you need to try.

5

I work in a big city during the week, so it's nice to come home here in the evening and relax after work. It's very quiet and there aren't many things to do, but there's a big city only 30 minutes away by car.

UNIT 5   Recording 1

K = Kim   H = Harry

K: Hey, look at this Harry, it's my old school yearbook. Do you remember this?

H: Oh right, with all our photos from when we finished school. Wow!

K: That's right. And look, there's you. Oh Harry, look at that hairstyle!

H: Oh come on, lots of boys had long hair then.

K: Yeah, but it was green!

H: Ha ha! I know. Moving quickly on … so where are you?

K: Oh no, we don't need to look at –

H: Come on … oh, there you are! Kim, that's a good photo. You were very good-looking at school.

K: Oh, but not now? Thanks!

H: No, of course you are now, too!

K: Aww, thanks. I was very quiet at school though.

H: Hmm, maybe, but you were very hard-working. Which, of course, you are now, too. But you're not quiet now, you're

funny. Anyway, who else is there? What about your friend Luisa?

K: Let me see. Oh, here she is.

H: Oh my, look at those clothes! Aren't they funny? I don't think she liked me. She wasn't friendly to me at all, she always called me names.

K: Oh, I don't think so. She wasn't very friendly to anyone. She was just very quiet. She's different now though, she's got a really interesting job and she's very kind.

H: So, who else is there? Do you remember that boy with long blonde hair? He was always at the back of the class and he was very quiet.

K: Oh yes, Shaun? Here he is. All of the girls liked him. He had these beautiful blue eyes …

UNIT 6   Recording 1

C = Connor   R = Rachel

C: It's my dad's 60th birthday this year and I don't know what to buy him.

R: What does he like?

C: Well, when they were young, my parents really liked camping, you know staying in a tent in the countryside. We always went on camping holidays when I was a child. But he's too old to stay in a tent now.

R: What about a 'glamping' experience?

C: A … what?

R: Glamping. It's like camping, but it's really comfortable. I went glamping with my husband last summer. He bought me a glamping weekend as a birthday present.

C: Oh yeah? What did you do?

R: Well, we arrived there around 2 p.m. and the manager showed us our tent. Well, I say tent, but it was more like a nice hotel room!

C: Why was that?

R: It was really big inside, you could walk around. And it was luxury. There was a real bed, a fire, a TV … even a little kitchen.

C: Really? Did you cook?

R: Ha! No, we didn't. It was my birthday! Actually, we just sat outside in the afternoon, then we ate out in town.

C: What did you eat?

R: Italian food. I had pasta and my husband had chicken.

C: What did you do the next day?

R: The next morning we woke up quite early, had breakfast, then walked along the river. It was beautiful. Then we drove to a little restaurant and had lunch.

C: When did you leave?

R: We left just after lunch, at twelve o'clock.

C: So, did you like it? Was it a good experience?

R: Definitely. It was really nice to stay in the countryside, but in a comfortable way, you know?

C: That's a great idea for a present. My mum and dad can stay there together. Thanks Rachel!

P = Presenter   J = Jeff

P: Hi, I'm Christine Evans and welcome to today's episode of *Life and Times*. With me in the studio today is Jeff Baines, who grows a lot of his own food at home. So, Jeff, what exactly do you grow?

J: Almost everything. I grow lots of vegetables, things like potatoes, beans, that kind of thing. I also grow some fruit, mainly apples, and some oranges. I grow herbs in the kitchen, too. I love cooking with them because they make my meals taste much better.

P: What about meat? Are you a vegetarian?

J: Well, I don't eat a lot of meat, but I'm not really a vegetarian. I've got a few chickens and they give me fresh eggs every day.

P: So, do you grow everything you need?

J: Oh no, not everything. There are a few things I buy, like milk, sugar and sometimes some sweets or cakes. But I think I make the majority of what I eat. It's definitely cheaper than buying all my food.

P: That's amazing. How did you start?

J: Well, a few years ago I moved to a new house and I saw that the garden got a lot of sunlight in the day. So I decided to plant some tomatoes. That first summer they grew really, really well and I had hundreds of tomatoes. I had tomato soup, tomato sauce, tomato salads ... By the end of the summer I didn't want to see another tomato ever again!

P: Ha! Yes, I can imagine.

J: So, the next year I tried a few different vegetables, and they all grew really well, too. Every year I grow more and more.

P: Why do you do it?

J: Well, I think it's important to grow your own food. Some people do it because it's cheaper than buying it all in supermarkets, and this is true, but it's not why I do it. For me it's a wonderful feeling to eat food that I know I cared for and loved myself. It's also good to control what you grow and what you eat so that you don't waste or throw away food.

P: Thanks Jeff. And one last question: do you still grow tomatoes?

J: Ha! Just a few.

P = Presenter   K = Kevin

P: Next we're talking to Kevin Anderton, a 33-year-old office worker from the UK. At the moment, Kevin is cycling around the world and he's kindly agreed to take some time out to speak to us. Kevin, welcome. Where are you at the moment?

K: Hi, I'm staying in a small town in the north of Argentina at the moment. The weather isn't great – it's raining a lot – so I'm having a break from the trip for a day or two.

P: Oh, that sounds like here in London. It's cold and raining here! So, Kevin, why did you decide to cycle around the world?

K: Well, it all started a few years ago. I had a boring desk job and I realised I didn't want to sit in front of a computer for eight hours a day at work. I really wanted to see the world and I love cycling, so I thought, why not?

P: What's a typical day for you?

K: Well, as I said, I'm not cycling at the moment, I'm enjoying the local food and culture. But I usually get up around 5 a.m. and have breakfast. It's important to eat well because I need the energy, but I can't eat too much. Then I just get on my bike and go!

P: How far do you cycle each day?

K: It depends where I am, what the weather's like, that kind of thing. I try to cycle at least a hundred kilometres a day though. The most I travelled in one day was two hundred and five kilometres. That was cycling down a mountain, so it was easier.

P: Wow, that's a lot! Where do you sleep?

K: I usually sleep outside, so I try to travel in the summer months when the weather is warm. I really enjoy a camp fire and having dinner outside at the end of a long day of cycling.

P: Yeah, that does sound nice. So, finally, what advice can you give for someone who wants to cycle around the world?

K: Start small. Maybe go for a ride at the weekend near your home and sleep outside in a tent. Try it and see if you like it. Then, maybe go on a short cycling holiday. The best thing about travelling like this is that you experience the environment, people and culture in the best way. You get close to the environment and the people. I love it!

P: Great, thanks for sharing your experience with us Kevin and good luck with the rest of the trip!

K: Thank you.

C = Chris   M = Magda

C: So, I think I might try this new diet.

M: Oh, really? What is it?

C: It's called a ketogenic diet, or 'keto'. Basically you eat lots of fat – things like oil, meat, cheese, that kind of thing.

M: OK.

C: Then you eat very little food with carbohydrates – things like sugar, bread, pasta.

M: Hmm, I don't think that's a good idea. It sounds like a fad to me.

C: A fad? What do you mean?

M: You know, a diet that gives you good results quickly, but it's difficult to continue for a long time. They can also be pretty unhealthy.

C: I see what you mean. Hmm, I guess this diet does sound a bit unhealthy. Also, I love bread!

M: I know you do!

C: So, what should I do?

M: Well, I think you should change more than your food. Think about the long term. Find something that works for you. Do more exercise. Maybe start a new sport or hobby.

C: Maybe I could go cycling?

M: Yes, why don't you cycle to work? That way it can be part of your everyday routine.

C: That's a great idea.

M: You should eat what you want, too, but try eating less, have smaller meals. You can use an app to record what you eat, that really helps, I think.

C: Good idea. Thanks Magda, that's really good advice.

M: You're welcome!

P = Presenter   S = Scott   A = Amelia

P: Hello, and welcome to *Techworld*. I'm here as usual with
    Scott and Amelia and today we're discussing the question,
    'Do we communicate more or less with modern technology?'
    So, Scott, what do you think?

S: Definitely less. My teenage son is really into video games.
    He just stays in his bedroom all evening. He never talks to us!

P: Amelia, do you agree?

A: Not really. Scott, your son is probably playing games
    online and talking to people all over the world. So he's
    communicating more than usual.

S: But it's not the same. When I was his age, I spent time with
    my friends, having conversations and going out, talking to
    people. I don't think it's healthy to stay inside your bedroom
    all the time, playing games.

A: Have you ever played an online game, Scott?

S: No, I haven't.

A: There's a lot of communication in games. You often have to
    speak to different kinds of people all around the world. So
    you actually communicate with people more than we did
    when we were his age.

S: Hmm … .

A: And it's not just online games. Social media is also important
    because we can meet people from all over the world and
    actually make new friends. In fact, I know someone who
    got married to someone they met on social media! Without
    modern technology that wouldn't be possible.

S: I understand, but I think the quality of communication these
    days is worse. For example, we don't have long telephone
    conversations and connect with people in the same way. We
    just send a quick text message with important information.
    We don't ask, 'How are you?', 'How was your day?'. There's no
    small talk. These things are important because they help us
    connect to the people we know.

A: Maybe, but we do connect with a lot of new people, more
    than before.

P: OK, well two very different opinions there. So, listeners,
    what do you think? Call us or send us an email and tell us
    your thoughts.

ANSWER KEY

UNIT 1

 1A

1
1 is 2 'm 3 aren't 4 're 5 is 6 isn't 7 are 8 isn't

2
1 Gin and Ken **are** from Scotland.
2 Pedro **isn't** from Argentina. He's from Brazil.
3 My name**'s** Anna. I'm from the Frankfurt office.
4 Where **are** you from?
5 I think they **are** Vietnamese.
6 We**'re** Australian, not British.
7 My town **is** about 30 kilometres from Warsaw.
8 John and Trina **are** from the same town.
9 It**'s** nice to meet you.
10 She **isn't** a student.

3
1 Karen's from Nigeria.
2 They're in my class.
3 I'm from London.
4 It isn't our first time here.
5 They aren't students.
6 It's cold in here.
7 I'm not happy.
8 You aren't very tall.

4
1 the US 2 Chinese 3 Turkish 4 Australia 5 Egypt
6 Polish 7 Greek 8 Brazilian 9 Japan 10 Russia

5
1 Australian 2 Greek 3 Spanish 4 Japanese 5 Mexican
6 Chinese 7 Russian 8 Egyptian

6
1 Mexican 2 Greece, Greek 3 Poland, Chinese
4 Japan, Egypt 5 Russia

 1B

1
1 What's 2 Where 3 When 4 Who 5 How 6 Are
7 What's 8 Is

2
1 How 2 Where 3 Are 4 When 5 What 6 Who
7 What 8 How

3
1 c 2 a 3 f 4 g 5 b 6 e 7 h 8 d

4
1 Are you on the Chinese course?
2 What's your email address?
3 When are the classes?
4 Is she the manager?
5 How are you today?
6 Are you interested in photography?
7 When is your birthday?
8 Are you a shop assistant?
9 Is Harry at home?
10 Where is your teacher from?

5
1 What's your phone number?
2 What's your job?
3 Where's Paulo?
4 Where are they from?
5 What's your favourite food?
6 When/What time are the classes?
7 What class are you in?
8 Is Sheila here?

 1C

1
1 ring 2 skateboard 3 sunglasses 4 board games 5 bike
6 laptop 7 tennis racket 8 camera 9 umbrella 10 picture

2
for studying: laptop
for playing/sport: skateboard, board games, bike, tennis racket
for wearing: ring, sunglasses

3
1 board game 2 bike 3 laptop 4 camera

4
1 this 2 that 3 these 4 those

5
1 that 2 those, these 3 This 4 that 5 that, This, that
6 those

6
1 These sunglasses are from Italy.
2 Is that your bike?
3 This picture is nice.
4 Is that Mike over there?
5 How much is that book?
6 Hi, Sundeep. This is Ben.
7 How much are these board games?
8 This bag is £50.
9 Is this your pen?
10 That lamp isn't Chinese.

 1D

1
1 c 2 a 3 e 4 b 5 d

2
1 is it, half 2 the, o'clock 3 's, quarter 4 What, four twenty
5 there, past 6 in, a.m.

3
1 It's four twenty. It's twenty past four.
2 It's nine forty-five. It's a quarter to ten.
3 It's one thirty. It's half past one.
4 It's seven fifty-five. It's five to eight.
5 It's five thirty. It's half past five.
6 It's two twenty-five. It's twenty-five past two.
7 It's three fifteen. It's a quarter past three.
8 It's eleven thirty-five. It's twenty-five to twelve.

Listening

1
a 3 b 2 c 1

2

Italy, Spain, Spanish, Australian, American, the UK, British, Mexico, Mexican

3b

1 T   2 T   3 F   4 F   5 T   6 F

4

1 b   2 d   3 a   4 c

Reading

1

a 3   b 2   c 4   d 1

2

a 2   b 3   c 1   d 4   e 3   f 2   g 4

3

1 F   2 T   3 F   4 F   5 T   6 T   7 F   8 T

4

1 improve   2 social programme   3 exciting   4 lake   5 boating

Writing

1

your favourite object; a photo

2

1 Brazil   2 ten years old   3 because it goes everywhere with her
4 Sandra   5 No, it's quite small.

3

at the beginning of a sentence; the subject I; people's names;
road or street names; names of towns, cities, states and countries;
nationalities

4

These are my board games. I love playing them with my friends.
Every Wednesday evening we play them together at a club in
Woodhall University on Green Street. They are all English.
My friend Raed is very good at them.

UNIT 2

 2A

1

1 father   2 parents   3 daughter   4 mum   5 children
6 grandfather   7 grandma   8 son

2

Male: father, grandfather, son
Female: daughter, mum, grandma
Both: parents, children

3

1 mum   2 grandchildren   3 uncle   4 parents   5 children
6 grandad/grandfather   7 nephew   8 grandparents

4

1 John is Alice's grandad.
2 Vera and Alfie are Mark's grandparents.
3 My parents' house is quite big.
4 My dad's dad is called Harry.
5 What's your mother's name?
6 Is Kira Jean-Luc's sister?
7 Her son's name is Chris.
8 Is that Briana's bike?
9 My grandparents' dog is called Poppy.
10 My brother's name is Damiano.

5

1 your, Rachel's   2 brother's, His   3 Stan Michelle's, her
4 Brian's   5 your, Tanya's   6 your, it's

6

1 My   2 her   3 its   4 His   5 Our/My   6 Their   7 your

2C

1

1 purse   2 driving licence   3 sweater   4 phone charger
5 hairbrush   6 necklace   7 make-up   8 earrings   9 notebook
10 handbag   11 gloves   12 scarf

2

P	S	W	E	R	T	A	E	A	R	R	I	N	G	S	S
C	R	E	W	Q	N	O	T	E	B	O	O	K	G	G	S
S	W	E	A	T	E	R	N	O	T	O	O	S	K	S	
H	A	N	B	D	C	V	O	R	S	T	I	P	P	J	
E	C	K	L	A	K	E	E	P	U	G	E	R	H	C	
H	A	R	L	I	L	U	P	S	A	R	F	P	O	H	
H	A	N	D	B	A	G	J	X	D	R	I	V	N	A	
H	A	I	R	B	C	U	S	H	K	A	B	L	E	R	
W	A	I	S	T	E	M	A	K	U	P	H	A	C	G	
G	O	V	E	L	M	A	K	E	U	P	A	S	H	E	
P	G	L	O	V	E	S	F	I	O	U	S	W	A	H	
U	S	W	E	T	R	E	I	E	A	R	E	I	R	A	
R	U	N	H	A	I	R	B	R	U	S	H	T	G	N	
D	R	I	V	I	N	G	L	I	C	E	N	C	E	D	
S	U	C	H	U	S	H	A	R	F	S	C	A	R	F	

3

sweater, necklace, make-up, earrings, handbag, gloves, scarf

4

1 mine   2 yours   3 Whose, Jack's   4 hers   5 Whose, ours

5

1 This make-up is theirs.
2 Those earrings are Sally's.
3 Whose wallet is this?
4 CORRECT
5 This cap is mine, but that one's yours.
6 These gloves are mine.
7 Is this ours?
8 CORRECT
9 These notebooks are theirs.
10 This laptop charger is ours.

6

1 They're hers.   2 That's his.   3 Is this yours?   4 It's theirs.
5 Are these mine?   6 Those are yours.   7 It's hers.
8 Are they ours?

2C

1

1 soft   2 an old   3 broken   4 special   5 beautiful
6 comfortable   7 light   8 round   9 useful   10 gold

2

1 laptop   2 earrings   3 board game   4 umbrella   5 bike

3

1 modern   2 light   3 large

4

1 's   2 haven't   3 Have you   4 haven't   5 haven't got
6 's   7 Have   8 has   9 Have we   10 haven't

5

1 We haven't got a large car.
2 Sara's got a bag with her.
3 He's got a car, but he hasn't got a bike.
4 I haven't got a camera with me.
5 My flat has got a garden.
6 I haven't got time now.

6

1 A: Have you got a car?
B: No, I haven't. But I've got a bike.
2 A: Have they got a garden?
B: Yes, they have.
3 A: Has she got any brothers or sisters?
B: Yes, she has. She's got two brothers and one sister.
4 A: Have you got the password?
B: No, I haven't. Sorry.
5 A: Has Scott got any pets?
B: Yes, he has. He's got a dog.

2D

1

1 got 2 like 3 much 4 are 5 change 6 Have 7 where
8 else 9 Can 10 Cash 11 Would

2

1 f 2 a 3 g 4 h 5 c 6 j 7 b 8 e 9 i 10 d

3

1 C 2 A 3 A/C 4 C 5 A 6 A 7 C 8 A 9 A 10 C

Listening

1

1 Henry, his cat 2 herself (Jeanette)

2

1 B 2 R 3 J 4 R 5 J 6 J

3b

1 ten 2 mum 3 three 4 four 5 cousins 6 likes

4

1 c 2 a 3 b

Reading

1

c

2

1 cables, a printer, a sofa and chairs
2 an engineer, a student, a young person in a new home
3 clearitfindit.com
4 It's free.
5 new, free, easy to use, useful
6 thousands

3

1 F 2 T 3 F 4 T 5 F

4

1 contact 2 cables 3 sofa 4 post 5 broken 6 steps
7 members

Writing

1

A notebook B laptop C scarf D bike

2

B Lost laptop! I have lots of exams to study for, so I need to find it. It's a 'Factbook' and it's silver and blue.
C It's a beautiful scarf. It's green and it's very soft and comfortable. It's cold now, so I need it to keep warm!
D It's a large men's bike. It's green and black and very fast. It's not new, but it's expensive. I use it to go to work every day and I don't have a car, so I need to find it.

3

1 (c) It's not expensive, but it's important to me.
2 (f) It's cold now, so I need my sweater.
3 (a) They're gold and (they're) beautiful.
4 (e) My bike is large and (it's) heavy.
5 (b) My laptop is broken, so it's not useful.
6 (d) They're not beautiful, but they're comfortable.

UNIT 3

3A

1

1 read 2 meet 3 play 4 do 5 cook 6 go 7 go
8 watch 9 paint/draw 10 visit

2

1 play 2 watch 3 go 4 read 5 meet 6 visit 7 cook
8 Go

3

1 meet 2 visit 3 go 4 watch 5 paint/draw 6 read
7 cook

4

1 I often go out with friends.
2 We don't watch TV in the morning.
3 You never cook on Fridays.
4 The children go online in the evening.
5 We visit a museum once a month.
6 You always have pizza!
7 I cook dinner for my family every night.
8 They don't have a lot of free time.
9 We often do a lot of sport.
10 I rarely read newspapers – I don't have time!

5

1 I often go out at the weekend.
2 We rarely watch sport on TV.
3 You sometimes cook dinner.
4 They go for a walk every day.
5 I read a lot of books.
6 I rarely watch TV in the afternoon.
7 They often make pasta for dinner.
8 I meet my grandma every Saturday.
9 We don't have a lot of free time at the weekend.
10 I hardly ever go online in the evenings.

3B

1

1 go 2 get 3 do 4 get 5 have 6 go 7 go 8 get
9 leave 10 do 11 start 12 have

2

1 b 2 e 3 h 4 a 5 f 6 g 7 c 8 d

3

1 have 2 goes 3 does 4 get 5 have 6 get 7 gets
8 go 9 leave

4

1 Sara **watches** TV every evening.
2 She **gets up** early in the morning.
3 Paulo **doesn't** have breakfast in the morning.
4 He **carries** a big bag with him at work.
5 We **play** video games together.
6 Sheena **loves** her job.
7 I **start** work at 9 a.m.
8 Chiara **doesn't go** to the gym.
9 I like action films, but she **doesn't** like them.
10 We **don't** have dinner together.

5

1 gets up 2 doesn't have 3 has 4 leaves 5 gets
6 starts 7 loves 8 has 9 finishes 10 goes 11 start
12 says 13 say

3c

1

1 Do 2 Does 3 does 4 do 5 do 6 does 7 does 8 do
9 do 10 Does

2

1 Do, don't 2 Does, does 3 Do, do 4 Does, does
5 Does, doesn't

3

1 How often do you go to the gym?
2 Where does Alessandra live?
3 How old is she?
4 What do you do at the weekend?
5 Where does she meet friends?
6 Where does John work?
7 What's your favourite food?
8 What does he do? / What's his job?
9 Are you interested in football?
10 Who's your favourite actor?

4

1 the radio 2 the theatre 3 the piano 4 games online

5

1 watch 2 listen to 3 visit 4 plays 5 go to 6 watch
7 go to 8 watch

6

1 go 2 play 3 play 4 meets 5 go 6 watches 7 read
8 go

3d

1

1 can 2 like 3 Which 4 out 5 available 6 sit 7 the
8 are

2

1 much 2 tickets 3 together 4 aren't 5 that's 6 Here

Listening

1

He rests.

2

a 3 b 6 c 1 d 8 e 2 f 7 g 4 h 5

3b

1 b 2 a 3 b 4 a 5 a

4

1 b 2 d 3 a 4 c

Reading

1

b

2

1 F 2 T 3 T 4 F 5 F 6 T 7 F 8 T

3

1 Sarah 2 Sarah 3 Jess 4 Jess 5 Sarah

4

1 a 2 a 3 a 4 b

Writing

1

Saturday

2

1 go out with friends
2 because she plays football on Saturday morning
3 about three hours
4 her mum
5 because it's cheap
6 She goes to the gym.

3

University life isn't … ; but I don't … ; On Friday evenings، … ;
on Saturday mornings، … ; In the afternoon، … ; It's not very
exciting … ; After that، … ; In the summer، … ; In the winter، … ;
so I'm ready …

4

1 That's a nice cap.
2 I get up, have a shower and make breakfast.
3 Those are Alice's sunglasses.
4 My friends' names are Claire and Vicki.
5 On Saturday mornings, I sleep late.
6 I don't like fish.

UNIT 4

4a

1

Across
2 shops 4 castle 5 offices 7 police station 8 garage
9 stadium 11 bus station 12 train station
Down
1 theatre 3 post office 6 sports centre 10 car park

2

1 post office 2 shops 3 theatre 4 train station
5 bus station 6 castle 7 garage 8 stadium
9 sports centre 10 offices

3

1 any 2 's 3 aren't 4 a 5 's 6 some 7 a

4

1 There aren't any offices in my town.
2 There are some shops near my house.
3 Are there any shops in your village?
4 There isn't a post office near me.
5 There isn't a police station in my town.
6 Is there a train station in your town?
7 There are a lot of shops.
8 There's a garage over there.
9 Are there any good shops in your town?
10 Is there a car park near the bank?

5

1 There are a lot of museums in London.
2 There aren't any places for young people.
3 There's a cinema in my town.
4 There isn't a police station near here.
5 There's a train station next to my office.
6 There isn't a theatre in my city.
7 There aren't any garages in this area.

4b

1

1 curtains 2 bath 3 furniture 4 cupboard
5 shower 6 garden 7 wardrobe 8 garage

2
1 cupboard 2 curtains 3 shower 4 upstairs 5 garage
6 wardrobe

3
1 garden 2 curtains 3 cupboard 4 garage 5 furniture
6 downstairs 7 wardrobe 8 fridge

4
1 the 2 a 3 a, The 4 a 5 the 6 a 7 a, the 8 the
9 – 10 a, the

5
1 the, the 2 the, the 3 a, a, the 4 –, the 5 The, the

6
We don't have **a** big house, but it's really nice inside. There are two bedrooms: **a** big one and **a** small one. **The** big one is where I sleep and **the** small one is **a** spare room. Downstairs, there's **a** living room and **a** kitchen. **The** living room is really bright. But my favourite thing about my house is **the** garden. It's really big and in **the** summer I like to sit outside and listen to music.

4c

1
1 b 2 c 3 e 4 a 5 f 6 d

2
Things you use to eat/drink: bowl, knife, water bottle
Things you wear: boots, gloves, hat, sunglasses, warm clothes

3
1 hat 2 sunglasses 3 map 4 warm clothes 5 backpack
6 water bottle 7 batteries 8 blanket 9 can 10 gloves

4
1 You need to take a map.
2 We need some eggs.
3 I need some warm clothes.
4 She needs a new laptop.
5 I need to get some sleep.
6 We need to start a fire.
7 I need some batteries.
8 You need a blanket.
9 We need to leave soon.
10 I need to get some water.

5
1 a 2 some 3 needs 4 to 5 some 6 to tell 7 a 8 to

6
1 I need to call my mother.
2 We need to buy (some) food.
3 They need to find a new house.
4 I need to get up early.
5 He needs to study.
6 I don't need any money.

4d

1
1 Where are the changing rooms?
2 What time does the museum close?
3 Is the museum free?
4 Can I take photos in the museum?
5 Where do I pay?
6 What time does the film end?
7 Is there a bank near here?
8 Are there any toilets near here?
9 How much is a ticket?

2
1 f 2 a 3 g 4 c 5 e 6 b 7 d

3
1 there 2 time 3 How 4 Can 5 Is

Listening

1
a small town

2
1 F 2 T 3 F 4 T 5 T 6 F 7 T 8 F 9 F 10 F

3b
1 aren't 2 aren't any 3 hour 4 need 5 friendly
6 30 minutes

4
1 b 2 a 3 c

Reading

1
c

2
1 F 2 F 3 T 4 T 5 F 6 T

3
1 b 2 a 3 a 4 b 5 a

4
1 heating 2 tunnel 3 cruise ships 4 residents

Writing

1
to tell him about his home town

2
1 T 2 F 3 T 4 T 5 T 6 F

3
1 We'd love you … , It has everything you need, you like it, people watch films
2 a good idea, a small theatre, a big supermarket, a big cinema, local people, nice cafés , interesting shops, big parks, small sports clubs, a lovely place

4
1 I don't like my city.
2 People live and work there.
3 There are some great shops.
4 People have lunch in the park in summer.
5 I go to school with my friends every day.
6 Jamie plays football with his brother after school.

UNIT 5

5a

1
1 old 2 short 3 long 4 thin 5 grey 6 tall

2
1 hair 2 tall 3 big 4 thin 5 brown 6 blue 7 long
8 young

3
1 like, looking 2 hair, long 3 tall 4 do, eyes 5 tall, good

4

1 You are beautiful.
2 He's a very tall boy.
3 She's got long, dark hair.
4 Andrew's tall and thin.
5 My dad's short and fat.
6 She's a nice, old lady.
7 Alice has got big, blue eyes.
8 He's got a thin face.
9 Julia's a very tall woman.
10 My boss has got short, blonde hair.

5

1 She's a beautiful woman.
2 Mike looks tired today.
3 Janice has got beautiful, blue eyes.
4 My brother's a very tall man.
5 She's got long, blonde hair.
6 My dad's a tall man.
7 What does he look like?
8 My neighbour is tall and thin.
9 He's got really long hair.
10 He's a very good-looking man.

5B

1

1 awful 2 perfect 3 cool 4 great 5 horrible 6 nice
7 boring 8 interesting 9 terrible 10 lovely

2

Positive: perfect, cool, great, nice, interesting, lovely
Negative: awful, horrible, boring, terrible

3

1 boring 2 lovely 3 OK 4 brilliant 5 interesting 6 cool
7 interesting 8 terrible

4

1 were 2 Were 3 was 4 wasn't 5 was 6 weren't
7 wasn't 8 wasn't 9 were 10 was, were

5

1 was 2 were 3 were 4 wasn't 5 weren't 6 were
7 were

6

1 I was quiet when I was a child.
2 Who was your best friend at school?
3 My flatmates weren't at home last week.
4 Were your teachers funny?
5 Was she good at school?
6 Was your hair blonde when you were a child?
7 He wasn't very friendly yesterday.
8 Where were you last night?

5C

1

1 He can speak five languages.
2 She can play the guitar.
3 Can you count to ten in German?
4 I can't climb that tree.
5 We can all speak English.
6 They can't cook.
7 Can you play chess?
8 I can't swim very well.

2

1 Can, can't 2 can't, Can 3 Can, can 4 Can, can't
5 can, can't

3

1 James can play the piano, but he can't play the guitar.
2 Anna can't make bread, but she can make a good carrot cake.
3 I can speak English, but I can't speak French.
4 My dad can sing quite well, but he can't dance.
5 Max can't fix a car, but he can drive one!
6 I can say some words in Japanese, but I can't have a conversation.
7 She can't play an instrument, but she can sing beautifully.

4

1 b 2 h 3 g 4 i 5 c 6 d 7 j 8 a 9 f 10 e

5

1 speak 2 fix 3 cook 4 play 5 count 6 run 7 spell
8 bake

6

1 fix 2 play 3 spell 4 speak 5 bake 6 run 7 count
8 play

5D

1

1 b 2 f 3 h 4 a 5 g 6 d 7 e 8 c

2

1 Can you open the window?
2 Can I borrow your phone?
3 Could you open the door for me?
4 Could you help me with the washing-up?
5 Can I sit here?
6 Can you help me with something?, Can you get my laptop from my office?

Listening

1

four

2

1 green 2 good-looking 3 quiet 4 (very) hard-working
5 friendly 6 kind 7 long 8 blue

3b

1 T 2 F 3 F 4 T 5 F 6 T 7 T 8 F

4

1 c 2 a 3 b

Reading

1

1 b 2 d 3 a 4 c

2

Jane Harper: c, f
Gavin Fields: a, g
Catherine Williams: b, d
Joe Mattis: e

3

1 T 2 T 3 F 4 F 5 F 6 T

4

1 small talk 2 qualifications 3 details 4 typical 5 positive

Writing

1

b

2

1 She can speak eight languages.
2 sing a song using each language she knows

3

1 her background/childhood
2 a description of her now
3 her special skill

4

It was very funny! / I'm a bit quiet … I've got short blonde hair and blue eyes. / My special skill …

UNIT 6

 6A

1

1 c 2 a 3 b 4 a 5 c 6 c 7 a 8 b 9 c 10 c

2

1 Reena's Café is in the city centre.
2 I watched a film at my friend's house last night.
3 The children are outside, playing in the garden.
4 The shop's closed on Mondays.
5 The sports centre is next to the stadium.
6 My brother lives in London.
7 Is there a post office near here?
8 What do you usually do at the weekend?

3

1 studied 2 didn't 3 watched 4 didn't 5 finished
6 didn't study 7 missed 8 cried

4

1 played 2 wanted 3 didn't dance 4 cooked 5 didn't invite
6 painted 7 lived 8 didn't listen 9 talked 10 didn't study

5

1 was 2 called 3 invited 4 cooked 5 tried 6 talked
7 watched 8 laughed 9 studied 10 played

6B

1

1 b 2 k 3 d 4 i 5 a 6 e 7 l 8 j 9 g 10 h 11 c
12 f

2

1 went 2 bought 3 drove 4 left 5 sat 6 felt
7 woke up 8 saw

3

1 felt 2 sat 3 bought 4 left 5 brought 6 went
7 drove 8 made

4

1 b 2 a 3 a 4 b 5 a 6 b 7 b 8 a

5

1 had 2 missed 3 brought 4 felt, didn't go 5 bought
6 woke up 7 drove 8 didn't see 9 went 10 made

6

1 She caught a train to London.
2 She didn't have lunch with Sam.
3 She gave a presentation.
4 She had dinner with Jenny.
5 She didn't phone Lucas.
6 She didn't drive to Manchester.
7 She bought a new watch.
8 She didn't go to the theatre.
9 She didn't go to the gym.
10 She met Carla.

6C

1

1 with 2 with 3 to 4 to 5 as 6 to 7 to 8 with
9 to 10 to

2

1 with 2 to 3 as 4 to 5 to 6 to 7 with 8 to
9 with 10 to

3

1 When do you listen to music?
2 I walk to work every day.
3 Who did you talk to at the party last weekend?
4 Colin worked as a bus driver when he was younger.
5 Sally went to a girls' school when she was a child.
6 They travelled to Italy by bus.
7 I meet up with my friends once a week.
8 They listen to the news on the radio every morning.
9 She lives with her sister in New York.
10 I moved to France when I was 10.

4

1 did 2 Did, did, Who 3 Did, didn't 4 Did, did 5 did
6 Did, did, What

5

1 Did you watch a film last night?
2 Where did you go to university?
3 Did you like your school?
4 Who did you meet up with last night?
5 Why did they walk to work?
6 What did you do last weekend?
7 Did you have a good time?
8 When did you talk to Adriana?

6

1 Did you have a good time on holiday?
2 Where did you go to school?
3 Did you play video games when you were a child?
4 Why did they leave early?
5 Did you talk to David last night?
6 Did they move to a big house?

6D

1

1 c 2 d 3 a 4 b 5 e 6 f

2

1 S 2 R 3 R 4 R 5 S 6 S

3

1 sorry, worries 2 afraid, That's 3 I'm, all 4 sorry, OK 5 so
6 afraid, No 7 I'm, worries 8 really, OK

Listening

1

1 b 2 yes

2

a 3 b 5 c 7 d 6 e 1 f 2 g 4

3b

1 f 2 c 3 a 4 b 5 g 6 d 7 e

4

1 c 2 b 3 d 4 a

Reading

1

1 d 2 a 3 b 4 c

2
1 difficult 2 activities 3 good 4 class 5 a lot of 6 new
7 needs to relax 8 safe

3
1 They've got everything they want or they haven't got any hobbies or interests.
2 before
3 You can do exercise and have fun.
4 an online guitar course or a sushi-making class
5 something new
6 You can enjoy it too.
7 a flying lesson, driving fast cars and 'survival' experiences
8 people who want something exciting or a thrill

4
1 thrill 2 introductory 3 fantastic 4 break

Writing

1
Italy

2
1 c 2 e 3 a 4 b 5 d

3
Do you remember we drank coffee and talked about our plans for the year?
Then we got back to the town and had that beautiful lunch by the river.
Then we were all tired and slept for the rest of the afternoon!

4
1 We had dinner and talked about our lives.
2 I went to the party and Chris talked to me.
3 My mum came round last night and cooked dinner.
4 Anita got up early and had breakfast.
5 Jamie ordered fish and Alice ordered chicken.
6 She looked at me and I smiled at her.
7 Lisa and Charles went out and watched a film.
8 Charlotte and I went to the museum and saw a dinosaur.

UNIT 7

 7A

1
1 chicken 2 soft drinks 3 meat 4 salad 5 coffee 6 fruit
7 beans 8 tea 9 eggs 10 juice 11 fish 12 vegetables

2
from animals: chicken, meat, eggs, fish
from plants: salad, fruit, beans, vegetables
drinks: soft drinks, coffee, tea, juice

3
1 fruit 2 frozen food 3 meat 4 juice 5 coffee
6 soft drink 7 pasta 8 vegetables

4
Countable: beans, eggs, soft drinks, vegetables
Uncountable: chicken, coffee, fish, frozen food, fruit, pasta, rice, tea

5
1 are 2 haven't 3 some 4 some 5 are 6 Is 7 isn't
8 any 9 some 10 a

6
1 Are 2 is 3 some 4 any 5 a 6 is 7 any 8 a
9 any 10 some

 7B

1
1 much 2 many 3 much 4 much 5 many 6 many
7 much 8 much

2
1 much, little 2 many, None 3 some, many 4 many, any
5 much, Lots 6 many, few 7 much, any 8 some, much, little

3
1 How many potatoes have you got?
2 We've got lots of/a lot of cheese.
3 We haven't got any coffee.
4 How much milk do you want in your tea?
5 We've got some bread, but we haven't got a lot of rice.
6 Can I have a few of your crisps, please?
7 I don't think there's any orange juice left.
8 We've still got a few tomatoes in the fridge.

4
1 c 2 a 3 i 4 e, j 5 f, g 6 h 7 b 8 d 9 g 10 j

5
1 carton 2 jar 3 box 4 tins 5 can 6 bottle 7 cup
8 bar

 7C

1
Across
6 comfortable 8 cool 9 fresh 11 crowded 12 bright
13 modern 14 dark
Down
1 nice 2 healthy 3 small 4 noisy 5 strange 7 expensive
10 popular

2
1 noisy 2 expensive 3 dark 4 popular 5 crowded
6 modern 7 strange 8 small

3
1 brighter 2 fresher 3 more expensive 4 noisier 5 larger
6 better 7 healthier 8 more delicious

4
1 Tom's Café is always more crowded than the River Café.
2 Canada is bigger than France.
3 My lunch is healthier than yours.
4 This café is much better than the old one.
5 The food here is much more expensive.
6 This car is smaller than your old one.
7 It's much nicer than I remember.
8 English food is worse than Italian.

5
1 Trains are faster than cars.
2 Salad is healthier than burgers.
3 Eating out is more expensive than eating at home.
4 This film is better than the first one.
5 Tokyo is bigger than New York.
6 Dogs are friendlier than cats.
7 Canada is colder than Egypt.
8 Sofas are more comfortable than chairs.

 7D

1
1 I'd like this sandwich, please.
2 Any hot drinks with that?
3 Can I get a large tea, please?
4 How much is that?
5 Eat in or take out?

2
a Take b I'd c in d like e Five

3
1 d 2 b 3 a 4 e 5 c

4
1 help 2 like 3 cold 4 that 5 Can 6 take 7 else
8 much 9 pay 10 over

Listening

1
b

2
1 T 2 F 3 T 4 F 5 T 6 T 7 F 8 F

3b
1 a 2 a 3 b 4 b 5 b 6 a

4
1 b 2 d 3 a 4 c

Reading

1
b

2
a 1 b 4 c 2 d 5 e 3

3
1 F 2 T 3 T 4 F 5 T 6 T 7 F

4
1 d 2 e 3 a 4 c 5 b

Writing

1
yes

2
1 because it sells real Mexican street food /
  because Guillermo is Mexican
2 vegetable tacos and a chicken burrito
3 because it's a food truck, not a restaurant
4 because Guillermo and the people who work with him are very
  friendly
5 because it's very popular (in the local area)
6 cheap and comfortable

3
We thought it was brilliant because the food is real Mexican street
food.
I think the food is delicious because it's all fresh.
It's also cheap because it's a food truck, not a restaurant.
It has a nice atmosphere because Guillermo and the people who
work with him are very friendly.
It gets crowded later in the evening because the food truck is very
popular in the local area.
I really like this place because it's cheap, comfortable and the food
is delicious!

4
1 b 2 a 3 e 4 d 5 f 6 c

UNIT 8

8A

1
1 countryside 2 sky 3 air 4 river 5 sea 6 trees
7 beach 8 water 9 island 10 mountain

2
1 c 2 a 3 b 4 a 5 a 6 c 7 b 8 a 9 b 10 a

3
1 water 2 river 3 beach 4 sky 5 countryside
6 mountain 7 air 8 island 9 trees 10 sea

4
1 I'm having dinner.
2 Gillian's playing football at the moment.
3 My parents aren't working today.
4 What are you doing?
5 We aren't doing anything.
6 Is Simon watching TV?
7 I'm standing at the top of the mountain.
8 Jamie and Kendra are leaving right now.

5
1 I'm walking to work at the moment.
2 Theo's swimming in the sea.
3 I'm really not/I'm not really enjoying this film.
4 She's eating a sandwich.
5 Where are you going now?
6 Yes, I'm driving back now.
7 Are you having a good time?
8 I think she's running on the beach.

8B

1
nouns: autumn, spring, summer, winter
verbs: raining, snowing
adjectives: foggy, hot

2
1 a 2 b 3 a 4 b 5 a 6 b 7 b 8 a

3
1 winter 2 sunny 3 foggy 4 windy 5 autumn
6 raining 7 hot 8 summer 9 cold 10 cloudy

4
1 d 2 a 3 h 4 c 5 f 6 g 7 b 8 e

5
1 are you doing 2 drive 3 go 4 'm having 5 's snowing
6 do you get up 7 are playing 8 don't do

6
1 do, work 2 work 3 Do, like 4 're changing
5 're introducing 6 're learning 7 're working 8 work

8C

1
1 taxi 2 home 3 house 4 a city 5 somewhere by bus
6 bike 7 home 8 the airport

2
1 a 2 c 3 a 4 c 5 a 6 b 7 c 8 a 9 c 10 a

3
1 in 2 at 3 on 4 off 5 in 6 at

4
1 the oldest 2 the longest 3 the nicest
4 the most expensive 5 the busiest 6 the best
7 the healthiest 8 the most beautiful 9 the worst
10 the strangest

5
1 The easiest 2 the best 3 the cheapest
4 the most interesting 5 the most expensive 6 the worst
7 the noisiest 8 the busiest 9 the most delicious
10 The safest

6

1 My grandma is the nicest person I know.
2 The Nile is the longest river in Africa.
3 Rahma's is the most expensive restaurant in the city.
4 That hotel is the worst in New York.
5 Tokyo is the largest city in Japan.
6 This is the busiest time of day for us.
7 My daughter is the most beautiful girl in the world.
8 This is the biggest shopping centre in Europe.

8D

1

1 Could I book a taxi, please?
2 Sorry, can you say that again?
3 Thanks very much for your help.
4 Do you mean the table near the window?
5 Hello, Greenfields Surgery.
6 Can I make an appointment with Dr Sanders?
7 Sorry, I didn't hear that.
8 See you soon.

2

1 again   2 that   3 See, for   4 mean   5 Thanks, soon
6 hear   7 book   8 speaking, make

Listening

1

1, 3, 4, 7, 8, 10

2

a 3   b 8   c 1   d 10   e 7   f 4

3b

1 F   2 T   3 T   4 F   5 F   6 T   7 F   8 F   9 T   10 T

4

1 b   2 d   3 a   4 e   5 c

Reading

1

a

2

1 moonbows
2 Cappuccino coast
3 Catatumbo lightning
4 lenticular clouds
5 lenticular clouds, halos
6 moonbows, Cappuccino coast

3

1 T   2 F   3 F   4 F   5 T   6 F   7 F   8 F

4

a a full moon   b UFOs   c foam   d sunset   e turbulence

Writing

1

a recommendation for somewhere to visit in Croatia

2

1 because the weather is perfect
2 Plitvice Lakes
3 go hiking, enjoy the views, take a boat trip, see interesting
  plants and animals, go skiing in the winter
4 the whole day
5 the right clothes and shoes for hiking, some sun cream and a
  good hat
6 walk off the trails or swim in the lakes

3

use adjectives

4

1 delicious   2 awesome   3 delicious   4 very   5 wonderful
6 terrible

UNIT 9

9A

1

1 stay   2 eat   3 join   4 Go   5 walked   6 keep   7 Sit
8 do

2

1 d   2 a   3 f   4 g   5 h   6 e   7 b   8 c

3

1 fit, do, gym,
2 down, up, around, healthy, well

4

1 b   2 f   3 h   4 a   5 d   6 g   7 c   8 e

5

1 shouldn't   2 should   3 should   4 shouldn't   5 shouldn't
6 should   7 shouldn't   8 Should

6

1 We should take a present to the party.
2 Should I call Simone?
3 You shouldn't talk to Richard like that.
4 Should we leave early?
5 You shouldn't eat so fast.
6 She should do more exercise.
7 Should I ask Ines?
8 I shouldn't eat so much.

9B

1

1 She's going to buy a mobile phone.
2 They're going to be late.
3 We aren't going to get there on time.
4 Are you going to stay at home today?
5 She isn't going to work late.
6 I'm going to learn another language.
7 What time are you going to leave?
8 I'm not going to eat chocolate this month.

2

1 It isn't going to be easy.
2 Are you going to see Sam?
3 What time are you going to get up tomorrow?
4 James and Chiara are going to have lunch together.
5 We aren't going to be late, don't worry.
6 What are you going to do at the weekend?
7 I'm not going to do anything!
8 We're going to watch a film at the cinema.

3

1 It's going to rain at the weekend.
2 You're going to be late.
3 I'm going to try a new recipe.
4 We aren't going to have a holiday this year.
5 They're going to visit Bangkok next summer.
6 She isn't going to get married.

4

1 b   2 f   3 a   4 d   5 h   6 c   7 g   8 e

5

1 learn 2 doing 3 talk 4 look 5 save 6 buy 7 get
8 decide

6

1 get 2 learn 3 decide 4 save 5 talk 6 do 7 look
8 buy

9c

1

1 skiing 2 swimming 3 climbing 4 sightseeing 5 skiing
6 bowling 7 cycling 8 climbing

2

1 horse riding 2 sightseeing 3 surfing 4 swimming
5 shopping 6 cycling 7 climbing 8 snowboarding

3

1 want, like 2 don't, do you want 3 Would, want to
4 wants, does, like 5 would you, want

4

1 I don't want to go swimming.
2 Janice wouldn't like to watch a horror film.
3 He doesn't want to travel by bus.
4 I wouldn't like to go to Iceland.
5 They don't want to go to a museum.
6 I don't want to learn how to play the piano.
7 Paulo doesn't want to find a new job.
8 You wouldn't like to go to a salsa class.

5

1 I'd like to go to the cinema.
2 Sheila wants to go on holiday.
3 Do you want to come to my party?
4 My parents wouldn't like to eat sushi.
5 I wouldn't like to get up that early.
6 I want to learn how to cook.
7 My wife would like to visit Paris.
8 I don't want to try anything new.

9d

1

1 c 2 e 3 a 4 g 5 h 6 b 7 i 8 j 9 f 10 d

2

1 shall, Let's, idea, like, please
2 Where, think, time
3 join, busy, come, Yes

Listening

1

She advises him to do more exercise and to eat less.

2

1 T 2 F 3 F 4 T 5 F 6 T 7 F 8 T

3b

1 a 2 b 3 b 4 a 5 a 6 a

4

1 c 2 b 3 a

Reading

1

c

2

a 3 b 1 c 4 d 2

3

1 b 2 b 3 a 4 a 5 b 6 a 7 a 8 b 9 a 10 a

4

1 simple 2 challenging 3 take your time 4 race

Writing

1

He's going to visit London.

2

1 (for) two months
2 (at a school in) Fulham
3 study (English)
4 go sightseeing
5 have a coffee

3

1 Hi Simon,
2 How are things with you?
3 I have some exciting news to tell you about.
4 What about you? Are you going to be in London?
5 Bye for now.

4

a 5 b 3 c 2 d 1 e 4

UNIT 10

10a

1

1 b 2 d 3 f 4 g 5 e 6 a 7 c

2

1 wash up 2 do 3 tidy 4 cook 5 fix 6 share 7 clean

3

1 bills 2 for 3 room 4 bathroom 5 laundry 6 up
7 things

4

1 cleaning, doing, tidying, washing
2 doing, going, sitting, watching, doing
3 talking, working, being, doing, meeting, having

5

1 Do you like visiting museums?
2 What do you like doing at the weekend?
3 I don't like travelling by bus.
4 Farah doesn't mind cleaning the bathroom.
5 We love sitting in the park.
6 Do you mind opening the window?
7 My dad hates cooking.
8 What subject do you like studying at school?
9 Do they mind sharing the bills?
10 My parents don't like staying at home.

10b

1

S	T	C	A	I	N	T	T	R	A	N	S
T	R	A	I	N	E	R	S	R	J	S	O
A	R	P	I	N	E	O	F	Y	T	I	E
S	I	O	E	N	E	U	E	A	S	T	E
B	O	O	T	S	F	S	J	E	R	C	S
I	O	P	R	D	R	E	S	S	E	B	U
V	C	R	E	E	O	R	S	S	T	Y	I
O	J	I	R	T	M	S	S	H	I	R	T
H	E	L	M	E	T	N	C	O	R	E	T
Y	A	E	U	N	I	F	O	R	M	A	X
E	N	R	I	E	F	R	A	T	F	O	R
S	S	N	U	N	I	T	T	S	O	R	F

2

1 cap, helmet
2 trousers, jeans, shorts
3 boots, trainers
4 suit, dress, uniform

3

1 smart clothes 2 coat 3 tie 4 a suit 5 shorts
6 trousers 7 helmet 8 dress 9 jeans 10 uniform

4

1 have, have 2 Does, has 3 to get, have, don't
4 tidy, do I have 5 do you have, have to

5

1 have to do
2 has to drive
3 don't have to answer
4 have to wear
5 have to get up
6 doesn't have to practise
7 have to study
8 don't have to be
9 have to have
10 doesn't have to have

6

1 don't have to 2 have to 3 don't have to 4 don't have to
5 has to 6 have to 7 doesn't have to 8 have to 9 have to
10 doesn't have to

10C

1

1 save 2 file 3 website 4 go 5 go 6 online game
7 website 8 screen

2

1 a 2 b 3 a 4 a 5 b 6 a 7 b 8 b 9 a 10 b

3

1 website 2 save 3 tablet 4 play 5 read 6 own
7 download 8 message

4

1 I've never been to Alaska.
2 Have you ever made a video?
3 Kieran has finished the report.
4 I've never eaten Italian food.
5 Has she ever been to Brazil?
6 I've never eaten meat.
7 Have you seen this film before?
8 You haven't done the washing-up!
9 What have you done?
10 I've never won a competition.

5

1 Have you ever driven for longer than eight hours?
2 She has had a meeting with her manager.
3 I've never flown in a helicopter.
4 Have they been there before?
5 He's never tried Indian food.
6 I haven't finished my breakfast yet.
7 Myra has never run a marathon.
8 We've never gone fishing.

6

1 I've seen that film twice.
2 Have you ever ridden a motorbike?
3 I've never worked in a restaurant.
4 We've chatted online a few times.
5 Have you ever written a computer program?

10D

1

1 like, Thank 2 well, of 3 make 4 looks, like it 5 This, of
6 so

2

1 a 2 g 3 c 4 b 5 h 6 e 7 f 8 d

3

1 so, you 2 your, it 3 job, say 4 looks, you 5 always
6 well, That's

Listening

1

b

2

1 F 2 T 3 F 4 F 5 F 6 T 7 F 8 T

3b

1 a 2 b 3 b 4 b 5 a 6 a

4

1 b 2 c 3 a

Reading

1

a

2

a 3 b 1 c not needed d 2 e 4

3

1 F 2 T 3 T 4 F 5 F 6 T 7 T 8 F

4

1 whiteboard
2 communal areas
3 turn up
4 condiments

Writing

1

to ask her to recommend a course

2

1 playing pronunciation games
2 vocabulary activities, listening to songs in class
3 speaking in front of the class
4 studying grammar, speaking in small groups

3

I really liked studying with you …; I love playing pronunciation
games – I'm a big fan of games …; these are my favourite!;
I also really like the vocabulary activities …; I'm OK with studying
grammar, but; it's not my favourite thing; I don't mind studying it …;
I can't stand speaking …; I'm fine with speaking …; I'm into music;
I like listening to songs in class …; That's really good fun.

4

1 b 2 b 3 c 4 a 5 c 6 a

Pearson Education Limited
KAO TWO
KAO Park
Hockham Way
Harlow
Essex
CM17 9SR
England
and Associated Companies throughout the world.

english.com/roadmap

First published 2020

Seventh impression 2024

ISBN:978-1-292-22787-0

Set in Soho Gothic Pro

Printed and bound by CPI Group (UK) Ltd, Croydon, CR0 4YY

Image Credit(s)

Alamy Stock Photo: Hero Images Inc. 39, Jenny Bailey 26, Velomorvah 27; **Getty Images:** Betsie Van Der Meer 6, Blyjak 56, Caiaimage/Chris Ryan 38, Caiaimage/Paul Bradbury 23, 55, Caiaimage/Sam Edwards 63, CasarsaGuru 61, CoffeeAndMilk 28, Creatas 9, D3sign 40, DaveBolton 8, DGLimages 29, Djiledesign 7, Emilija Manevska 11, Eric Lin / EyeEm 41, Fbxx 24, FotoAta 15, Franklin Castillo 50, Georgeclerk 34, Hoxton/Tom Merton 58, 62, Izusek 18, 33, 53, Kali9 5, 17, Kiankhoon 38, Maskot 45, Micheyk 51, Mikroman6 52, MoMo Productions 10, Nicholas Free 25, NoSystem images 42, Pekic 20, PeopleImages 4, Ron Krisel 31, Ryan McVay 37, Simonkr 19, Svetikd 44, Tetra Images - Erik Isakson 54, Tom Werner 59, ValuaVitaly 12, Vichie81 14, Westend61 7, 30, 46, 49, William87 57; **Shutterstock:** Andrey_Popov 32, Arek_Malang 21, Joshua Resnick 43

Cover image: *Front:* **123RF.com:** Igor Plotnikov

Every effort has been made to trace the copyright holders and we apologise in advance for any unintentional omissions. We would be pleased to insert the appropriate acknowledgement in any subsequent edition of this publication.